Rüdiger

C000057283

111 Places
in Mallorca
that You Shouldn't
Miss

emons:

Bibliographical information of the Deutsche Nationalbibliothek
The Deutsche Nationalbibliothek lists this publication
in the Deutsche Nationalbibliografie; detailed bibliographical
data are available on the internet at http://dnb.d-nb.de.

© Emons Verlag GmbH
All rights reserved
© all photos: Rüdiger Liedtke, except:
page 19 Fundación Yannick Y Ben Jakober; page 41 Coves de Campanet;
page 83 Sofia Dobrzecki
Design: Eva Kraskes, based on a design
by Lübekke | Naumann | Thoben
Maps / Cartography: Regine Spohner
Printing and binding: B.O.S.S Druck und Medien GmbH, Goch
Printed in Germany 2014
ISBN 978-3-95451-281-2
Original title: 111 Orte auf Mallorca, die man gesehen haben muss
First English edition, translated from the German by Kathleen Becker

For the latest information about emons, subscribe to our free newsletter
at www.emons-verlag.de

Foreword

Why are there fish gasping for air in Palma's Cathedral, a house hanging precariously above a cliff, and people trying their luck in a former theatre? Did you know that in Santanyí you are close to the heavens, that the place to meet strong Mallorcan women is Artá and that Palma's city wall is graced by a bull? Would you care to be a guest of the archduke in Deiá, trace the founder of San Francisco in Petra, and meet the devil in Sa Pobla? In Palma you'll find a church that's upside-down, in Lluc the Ave Maria can be heard in other-worldly spheres, and time and again you'll encounter messages from the Knights Templar.

Mallorca is marked by its chequered past and a cultural variety that has few rivals. It has a unique landscape and one of Europe's most attractive cities, Palma de Mallorca, and the whole thing is suffused with the electrifying Mediterranean climate, no matter what time of year you choose to visit. Mallorca is so much more than sun, sand and the excesses of binge drinkers. The island has many different faces. You'll find mass tourism and exclusive 5-star hotels, pedal boats and luxury yachts, beach tennis and 18-hole golf courses. Many holiday-makers are drawn to the resorts right by the sea, while others prefer the remote »finca« in an olive grove, each enjoying the island in their own way. Yet they all share one thing: once they've »got« Mallorca, they'll never again talk about the island as a cheap and cheerful des-tination for the sun-starved masses. Far off the beaten tourist track, Mallorca offers plenty of surprises, both big and small, which will de-light whether you're on a short holiday or living on the island perma-nently, whether biker or hiker, sun worshipper or arts lover. This book will take even those familiar with Mallorca to places that will astound them: historical sites, hidden coves, secret spots, and oases of tran-quility far from the madding crowd. All 111 of them.

111 Places

1__ The Castell Miquel Winery

Viniculture at its finest

Getting here is a pleasure in itself. Passing the imposing rocky mountains of d'Alaró and de s'Alcadena on the road winding through the vineyards, you can see from afar, on an elongated building high on the hill, the lettering »Castell Miquel« with the white castle in front. The latter is the residence of the German pharmaceutical entrepreneur Prof Dr Michael Popp, who has set up a vineyard here creating wines that have gained a fine reputation and are now much more than an insiders' tip.

Specialising in natural remedies, and with a bestseller in Sinupret, the family-run Bionorica firm based in the little Bavarian town of Neumarkt has been taking advantage of the fantastic Mallorcan climate to grow medicinal plants for 15 years now, and runs a subsidiary processing plant in Costell.

At some point Michael Popp had the bright idea of buying the semi-derelict »Es Castellet« wine estate in the Tramuntana Mountains to rekindle viticulture here following scientific methods. Let's call it wine for medicinal purposes, produced organically. The former stables were converted into barrel storage rooms, maturing cellars and production spaces.

Today, the wine terraces of Castell Miquel, with their Syrah, Merlot and Cabernet Sauvignon, count amongst Mallorca's most exclusive slopes, which has led to some of the Castell Miquel wines being dubbed »Stairway to Heaven«. The winery is managed by a vintner from the Palatinate region of Germany.

While Castell Miquel has no restaurant there are regular wine tastings. Parties and events are also arranged on the extensive terraces of the winery, particularly when Bionorica are launching new plant-based remedies onto the market.

Address Bodegas Castell Miquel, Carretera Alaró–Lloseta, 07340 Alaró, tel. 971/510698, www.castellmiquel.com | Access from Palma Ma-13 in the direction of Inca–Port d'Alcúdia, exit Consell/Binissalem, then in the direction of Alaró, before you get to the centre of town head in the direction of Lloseta, at kilometre-mark 8.7 follow the »Bodega« sign | Opening times April–Oct Mon–Fri 11.30am–7.30pm, Sat 10am–2pm; Nov–March Mon–Fri 12 noon–5.30pm (with wine sale) | Tip A detour leads to the José L Ferrer vineyard in Binissalem with wine museum – well worth a visit and tasting.

2 __ The 13th Hole
Tee-off towards the islet

You don't have to be a golfer to take full advantage of this idyll. The incredible views, the clear air, the fabulous greenery and the fine restaurant with extensive terrace all conspire to make a visit to Alcanada Golf Club a pleasure.

Clubhouse and restaurant are located in a former finca – a Spanish country estate, or »ranch« – where you can have a drink or a bite to eat. Occupying a picturesque location on the La Victória peninsula in the northeast of Mallorca – those in the know reckon this to be the most beautiful golf course in the Balearics – this refuge, far away from it all, is a true insider tip.

The course is generously laid out and reaches well into the interior of the island, with hills and dales sloping down towards the sea and surrounded by a nature reserve bordering the Med. It offers views of faraway Alcúdia Bay, the mountainous panorama of the Sierra de Llevant and, first and foremost, the offshore Alcanada islet.

This small island with its white lighthouse, which functions to this day, lies some 100 metres off the coastline, below the golf course. The island can be accessed either by swimming, wading through the water or taking a boat.

Teeing off from the 13th hole sends the ball – assuming it was hit well – flying for what seems an eternity in the direction of the lighthouse.

Designed by the American golf course architect Robert Trent Junior, the Alcanada 18-hole links, just under 7 kilometres long, lies far from any source of noise pollution and is one of the island's couple of dozen more or less exquisite golf courses, most of which are situated in the Greater Palma area. All courses can be booked and played all year round simply by paying the green fee, no membership required.

Address Club de Golf Alcanada, Carretera del Faro–Alcanada, 07400 Port d'Alcúdia, tel. 971/549560, www.golf-alcanada.com | **Access** from Alcúdia on the Ma-3460, once in Port d'Alcúdia head for Alcanada, bus L 356 leaves from Port d'Alcúdia | **Opening times** All year round near-daily from 8am to dusk | **Tip** It's not far to Alcúdia's picturesque Old Town or into the bay of the same name with its long sandy beaches.

3__ The Can Torró Library

Bertelsmann's commitment to Mallorca

The Mohn family from Germany, owners of the Bertelsmann media empire comprising the publisher Random House, TV channel RTL and the widely read »Stern« magazine, have had a love of Mallorca for decades, owning a fine estate near Alcúdia. As the publishing group has always been pretty successful in Spain too, with the Spanish book club »Círculo de Lectores« one of their profitable ventures, the Mohns came up with the idea to erect a monument to themselves in Alcúdia.

Following the example of the municipal library in their home town of Gütersloh, a model institution was founded in 1989 in Alcúdia: the Can Torró Library.

Restored from the bottom up, the historic Casal Can Torró, which houses the library, is situated in the heart of the Old Town and has become one of the cultural centres of northeastern Mallorca.

Spread across three floors, Can Torró is not just a classic library and a place to promote reading, it is particularly strong in the multimedia activities that are so popular with pupils and students.

Alongside the classic literature, there are newspapers and magazines, games of all kinds and numerous well-equipped computer terminals where you can access the internet or check your emails.

Can Torró has become a meeting point in Alcúdia, but also a place of relaxation, with the large courtyard terrace particularly inviting.

While the town of Alcúdia has had sole responsibility for Can Torró since 1997, the Bertelsmann Foundation still maintains three people on the library's board of seven. The Fundacíon Bertelsmann, a satellite of the Bertelsmann Foundation, was founded in Barcelona with the aim of further developing library studies in Spain following Alcúdia's example.

Address Fundació Biblioteca d'Alcúdia Can Torró, Carrer Serra 15, 07400 Alcúdia, tel. 971/547311 | **Access** by public transport: Autocares Mallorca in the direction of Alcúdia centre, on foot a few metres from the Plaça de la Constitució | **Opening times** Tue–Sun 10am–2pm, Tue–Fri 4–8pm, closed Mon | **Tip** Neighbouring Can Fondo, dating back to the 14th century and immediately adjoining Can Torró, puts on regular contemporary art exhibitions and also houses the town's historical archive.

4__ The Hermitage La Victòria
For anyone who has always wanted to sleep in a monastery

Spending the night up here, at the top of the La Victòria peninsula, in one of the twelve monastic cells, is like travelling back in time to the Middle Ages. A visit to the hermit's cell of the Petit Hotel Hostatgeria La Victòria on the Cap of Pinar, with its fabulous views onto the Bay of Pollença and to Cap de Formentor, is also about contemplation. And in the evening, when the daytrippers – who come to see the Ermita de la Victòria below the former monastic cells of the Carmelites – have gone, you will sink into a meditative calm that you would hardly have suspected on Mallorca. Of course, the accommodation is monastically spartan, which also helps to keep prices down. And with this being a self-catering place, come 6pm you have to use your own key. The walls of this fortified convent are thick, the rooms small, and some of the windows minuscule. Yet the atmosphere it radiates, well run as it is, you will only find here at this place of pilgrimage.

Reached at the end of a narrow, winding road, Ermita de la Victòria dates back to the 13th century. The little church has given rise to many stories. One of them claims that shortly after the Reconquista a shepherd's boy found a statue of the Virgin Mary carved in wood, which ended up being venerated to the point of having this small chapel custom-built for it. In the 16th century, the statue kept being stolen by pirates, yet would always miraculously regain its original position at the altar. In this way the statue acquired its name, Mare de Déu de la Victòria, Our Lady of Victory, becoming a site of pilgrimage for Mallorcans on 2 July. Towards the end of the 17th century the interior of the church was redecorated and given three naves, a rounded vault and a baroque altar. In the early 18th century, and once more during extension work to the hotel occupying the two storeys above, the Ermita de la Victòria was again restored.

Address Carrer Cap des Pinar – Ermita de la Victòria, 07400 Alcúdia, tel. 971/549912 | Access from Alcúdia in the direction of Mal Pas or else Bonaire; the road to Cap of Pinar leads directly to the Ermita de la Victòria | Opening times In summer, the church is nearly always open in the daytime, and usually closed in winter. | Tip The Mirador del la Victòria restaurant above the church gives fine views. Below, only some 800 metres away, you'll find the small sandy swimming beach of S'Illot.

5_ The Jakober Collection
Children's portraits in an underground reservoir

Everything about this oasis of art is unusual, maybe even unique. The place is eccentric, the founders are true characters, and the collection itself is challenging. Hidden away on the La Victòria peninsula and only accessible by winding paths, the Fundación Yannick i Ben Jakober offers up a bouquet of surprises, which until recently seemed reserved for those in the know. This in itself is a surprise, as the cultural foundation set up by sculptors Yannick Vu and Ben Jakober has been in existence since 1993. But the collection housed in the Finca Sa Bassa Blanca, the »white lagoon«, built by Egyptian architect Hassan Fathy in 1978 in the Hispanic-Moorish style, has only really taken off in the past few years.

The portraits of children of the nobility are unmissable. Painted by Spanish, Flemish, English and French masters of the 16th to 19th centuries, and displayed in a former subterranean reservoir, the collection comprises some 150 of these historic children's portraits, which also served as »application« forms« for prospective marriages.

Contemporary art including work by Domenico Gnoli, Alan Rath and Meret Oppenheim is on view in one part of the main house. Separate rooms are dedicated to Rebecca Horn and Vu Cao Damon, one of the most famous Vietnamese artists of the 20th century and the Paris-based father of Yannick Vu. In 2007 the Socrates Hall was inaugurated, accessible by a large staircase from the park and boasting a very special mix of exhibits. Here you can see the fossil of a Siberian woolly rhinoceros dating back some 120,000 years in front of a Swarovski curtain seven metres wide and four metres high studded with 10,000 sparkling crystals, alongside work by Miquel Barceló and Gerhard Merz. It's also well worth visiting the extensive park with numerous large-scale granite animal sculptures created by the founding couple, who currently divide their time between Costa Rica and Mallorca.

Address Finca Sa Bassa Blanca, Es Mal Pas, 07400 Alcúdia, tel. 971/546915, www.fundacionjakober.org | **Access** Some 1.5 kilometres beyond Alcúdia, you reach the Mal Pas part of town. At the entrance to the area, turn right at the Bar Bodega des Sol into Cami de Muntanya, drive on for another 4 kilometres alongside the Alcanada golf club and follow signs to »Fundacíon«. If the gate is closed ring the bell. | **Opening times** Wed–Sat 11am–3pm, Thu 10am–12 midday, visits and guided tours by appointment only, Tue 9.30am–12.30pm and 2.30–5.30pm visits to the gallery and park without guided tour, closed Sun and Mon | **Tip** The two huge granite doves on the Plaça Porta de Santa Catalina in Palma were also sculpted by Ben Jakober.

6__ The Teatre Romà

Ancient Rome not far from the beach

In this small theatre, discovered in 1953 on the edge of the ancient Roman town of Pollentia and subsequently restored, the surrounding population would have been provided with light entertainment, theatre and dance – in a typical semi-circular Roman theatre with a stone grandstand, a large stage and platform for the orchestra. And all this in the first century AD. In contrast to most theatres of their kind the entire Teatre Romà was hewn into the rock. This might account for the fact that with a diameter of under 100 metres it is smaller than other comparable theatres of this style, although it still fitted some 2,500 visitors.

The Teatre Romà forms part of the town of Pollentia, founded in 70BC following the conquest of Mallorca by the Romans, not far from the town wall of what is today Alcúdia, and which became the cultural metropolis of the Roman province of Balearica. Today, the excavated ruins reveal the structure of the ancient town. Another excellent opportunity to explore more details from Alcúdia's Roman past is provided by the Museu Monogràfic de Pollentia in Carrer Sant Jaume.

In the 5th century AD, Pollentia finally bowed to the onslaught of the Vandals, who plundered the town, destroying most of it in the process. Its inhabitants fled, settling further north in what is today Pollença, naming it after their old capital and erecting a number of significant buildings, including the Pont Roma bridge, which are still standing. The ancient Roman town of Pollentia was never to recover again, parts of the land and the Teatre Romà being converted to the burial sites of early Alcúdia. Today's Alcúdia, and the name of the town itself, points back to the Moorish domination from the 10th century onwards. The town right next to the ruins of Pollentia had to wait until the 13th century and the Reconquista to develop into a larger settlement with church and town wall.

Address Avinguda Prínceps d'Espanya, 07400 Alcúdia, tel. 971/184211 | Access
on foot, along the Cami del Teatre Roma, parallel to the C-713 | Opening times
The theatre is always open. The Roman town of Pollentia and Monographic Museum:
Tue–Fri 10am–4pm, Sat, Sun 10.30am–2pm | Tip The modern arts centre Auditori
d'Alcúdia lies on Plaça de la Porta de Mallorca, just outside the preserved historic town
wall.

7_ The Glass Hut
The art of Spanish glass-blowing at the Gordiolas

Entering the Gordiola shop in Palma's Carrer Victòria, not far from the cathedral, gives you some idea of the high art of glass-blowing that awaits in the factory near Algaida. After all, the island enjoys a fine reputation in this craft. And you won't be disappointed. Coming from Palma, just before reaching Algaida you will hit the factory building inspired by a castle belonging to the Gordiola family, which has been running a glass-blowing operation here since the early 18th century. Young Bernado Gordiola had learned the art of glass-blowing in Venice and subsequently received a licence to establish his own glass-firing kiln. Ranking amongst the longest-established companies of its kind in Mallorca, Gordiola rose to be supplier to royal courts and palaces of the nobility all over Europe. Some 40 years ago, the family had the factory erected in the style of neo-Gothic industrial architecture. A little kitsch perhaps, yet somehow it fits the landscape.

Glass-blowing in Mallorca has a long tradition, going back to the time of the Phoenicians in the 2nd century BC. Settling the Mallorcan coastline, they brought their own glass-firing ovens and were already producing items of daily use. In the 16th and 17th centuries wealthy Mallorcan families would import their glass from Venice, the mecca of international glass-blowing. Until, that is, the Gordiolas arrived and worked alongside other artists to make the craft flourish in Mallorca too. The process is still as it was in the olden days, and visitors can watch the glass-blowers at work in the large open workshop space, as they shape vases, animal figures, chandeliers and many items of daily use from hot glass. The estate's courtyard leads into a small museum, displaying the private collection of the Gordiola family, with antique glass objects and exhibits of filigree glass painting. You can also buy glassware in Gordiola and while not exactly cheap, they are truly »Handmade in Mallorca«.

Address Carretera Palma–Manacor, 07210 Algaida, tel. 971/665046 | Access Take the minor road from Palma to Algaida, exit at km 19. | Opening times Mon–Sat 9am–7pm, Sun, Fri 9am–1pm | Tip Gordiola has two shops in Palma, in Carrer Victòria 6 and Jaime II 14. In Algaida, it's worth taking a look at Sant Pere i Sant Pau church and the restored windmills.

8__ The Jardí des Dones

A sculpture garden of strong Mallorcan women

It was some years ago that two ladies active in the women's movement created a monument to emancipation on Mallorca, but it has yet to be noticed by the wider public. This might be because the mission inspiring Gabriele Schilling and Christiane von Lengerke is that bit too specific.

The two Germans used their finca to set up a sculpture and arts garden telling the fascinating story of strong Mallorcan women along 20 stations – their »Jardí de les Dones Mallorca«, or Women's Garden.

Back in 1987 the two women bought the old finca, half-way between Artà and Can Picafort, untouched and off the road, together with the nearly 25,000 square-metre garden that came with it, and slowly started restoring the estate. Ten years later, the two friends, both already active in the German women's movement, moved onto their finca full-time and threw themselves into it, cultivating parts of the garden while deliberately leaving other corners to run wild. They dug a well, had power lines laid, and made the house completely habitable. And then the idea of the Women's Garden came up.

Between the many olive, almond and carob trees, they started developing a »Woman's History Trail«.

You'll meet George Sand, who, fascinated as she was by Mallorca, suffered through an entire winter at the side of Frédéric Chopin in Valldemossa. There's the contemporary Mallorcan writer Maria Antònia Oliver, literature professor Carmen Riera and singer Maria del Mar Bonet.

Discover the Mallorcan-born Communist activist Aurora Picornell, executed in her early years, as well as Catalina Homar, the emancipated lover of Archduke Ludwig Salvator. Every almond tree hides another homage to a strong woman.

Address Finca Ca Na Nofreta, Camí de Carossa, 07570 Artà, tel. 971/835023 or mobile 608/323511, http://jardidelesdones.mallorca.com | Access Ma-12 Carretera Artà–Can Picafort, exit at km 17.7 | Opening times for visits and guided tours phone ahead; closed in July, Aug, Dec | Tip The Ermita de Betlem hermitage is well worth seeing and accessible from Artà via the hairpin bends making up the Ma-3333.

9 The Stairway to Heaven

Sublime ascent to the Santuari de Sant Salvador

Visible from afar, the mountain of Artà with its old castle and pilgrimage church of Sant Salvador dominates this town of remarkable architectural unity. The way up the staircase lined by crosses leads to one of the most beautiful religious sites on Mallorca – the pilgrimage church of Sant Salvador. The best way to explore it is to start way down below from the narrow lanes of the small town. While certainly involving a bit of effort, this provides a special experience, particularly towards evening when the sun starts to go down, bathing the town in hues of gold, ochre and red. The way up to the mountain is signposted.

At the end of the narrow, steep Parroquia lane, you'll reach the late-Gothic fortified church of Transfiguració del Senyor, built in the 16th century on the foundations of a former mosque. Right behind the red-stone church marks the beginning of the Way of the Cross and its 180 steps, flanked by dense cypress trees, up to Sant Salvador, which proudly stands on the site once occupied by the Arabic Almudaina palace, chosen by Jaume I as his residence in 1229 following the conquest of this Islamic fortification.

The church of Sant Salvador was finally built in 1832 in the Renaissance style, developing over time into the religious centre for the citizens of Artà. The square in front of the church, enclosed by the fortified walls, is adorned by an impressive fountain surrounded by palm trees.

Inside the church, the faithful reserve their special adoration for a 17th century Virgin said to have repeatedly saved the inhabitants of Artà from pirate attacks. Other traditions date the wooden sculpture, with its elongated face and the infant Jesus on its lap, back to the 13th century. The paintings showing the handing over of Mallorca to King Jaume I by the Moors, and the stoning of Ramón Llull, are worth a look.

Address Carrer de Castellet, 07570 Artà | Access Past Artà, coming from Alcúdia via the Ma-12 or from Manacor via the Ma-15. Either go on foot from the centre of town up the steep stairs to the castle or drive to the church along the outer wall (signposted). There is a car park immediately in front of the castle wall. | Tip Right outside the town, Ses Païsses, a settlement of the prehistoric Talayot culture, awaits discovery. And those who'd like some more detail should explore the Museu Regional d'Artà on Plaça d'Espanya.

10___ The Terraces
Where the Moors left their indelible mark on the landscape

The grapes once cultivated here on a large scale, some of which are restored today, always enjoyed an excellent reputation, as did the wine they yielded. No wonder then that word of the small mountain village on the steep slopes of the Tramuntana range reached the Spanish mainland too.

Chroniclers tell that during the 13th-century reconquest of Mallorca from Moorish domination, Jaume I and his royal household supposedly took a particular shine to the terraced vineyards of Banyalbufar, as this was the place where the Malvasia grape reached full maturation and body, making this the wine of choice for the Aragon court.

The Moors managed to lay out mighty terraces supported by walls in this hard-to-tame landscape, in order to cultivate wine and farming.

The decisive factor here was a sophisticated irrigation system. Water basins would catch the water bubbling from sources deep within the mountain range, dividing it into small walled canals. Today's owners of the more than 1,000 terraces are still taking advantage of them. The very name Banyalbufar derives from Arabic, meaning something akin to »small wine garden by the sea«.

Banyalbufar was to acquire wealth and prosperity, and by the end of the 19th century counted amongst Mallorca's richest communities, as the Malvasia grape yielded the deliciously sweet dessert wines that were all the rage in Palma and Barcelona.

Then, around 1900, the phylloxera disaster spread across the island, destroying all Mallorcan vineyards, including those of this small mountain village. Mallorca had to wait until the 1980s to fully recover from this misfortune. Today, the village of 600 inhabitants is attempting to revive the Malvasia grape on these historic terraces.

Address 07191 Banyalbufar | Access from Palma take the Ma-1040 to Esporles, and continue on the Ma-1100 to the Ma-10 (Valldemossa–Andratx); by public transport: bus L 200 from Palma via Esporles | Tip Beyond Banyalbufar, in the direction of Andratx along the Ma-10 you'll hit one of Mallorca's most famous watchtowers, the 16th-century Torre del Verger. Visible from afar, it occupies a position on the outermost edge of the cliffs and offers a small viewing platform.

11__ The Italian Gardens
Take a stroll around a former palace of the nobility

For over three centuries, the Raixa manor house near Bunyola was in the possession of the Despuig family. When it was put up for sale in 2002, it attracted the attention of VIP buyers, with both Michael Douglas and Jil Sander eyeing up the picturesque estate. While the fashion designer offered a large sum for the country house, the island council made use of its purchasing prerogative and took possession of the property and park in order to make it accessible to the people too. A wise move, after Raixa had been off limits to the public at large for more than 30 years.

Raixa's origins lie in a 13th century Moorish finca which, following several changes of hands and conversions, came into the hands of the Despuig family in 1620. Its Italian aspects are due to a prominent son of the family clan. When Antonio Despuig y Dameto (1745–1813), a cardinal in Valencia with a flair for the fine arts, returned to Mallorca from a trip to Rome to visit the Holy See, it was clear to him that Raixa should be converted into an italian-style villa and the main house and huge gardens redesigned in the style of the Italian Renaissance. He was able to convince his brother Joan, the owner of Raixa, of the merits of this plan, and they set to work on creating an Italian landscape right in the heart of Mallorca.

The imposing group of houses clustering around the courtyard, with the central manor house and a loggia adorned by ten pillar arches, the outbuildings and mews, the olive press, wine cellar and chapel are surrounded by extensive gardens. At the centre of the ensemble, a freestanding neoclassical staircase leads up to the estate's own mountain with its numerous terraces and buildings, including an artificial grotto and a round temple built in 1854, with the insignia of the Despuig family. There is also the Apollo Garden and a large walled carp pond with a romantic terrace. Following years of intensive renovation work, parts of Raixa have been open to the public again since 2011.

Address Carretera Palma–Sóller, 07110 Bunyola, tel. 971 / 237636 | **Access** from Palma on the Ma-11 in the direction of Sóller, at km 12.2 before reaching Bunyola you'll see La Raixa on your left-hand side, bus L 210, L 211 Palma–Port d'Sóller, stop Bunyola or ask the driver beforehand to stop at the road to Caubet (Joan March hospital) | Opening times Sat, Sun 10am–2pm | Tip From Bunyola, it's worth taking the winding road to the mountain village of Orient.

12__The Bar Cala

At Antonia and Lorenzo's everything is as it was 50 years ago

Cala Figuera is proof that it is possible for time to stand still, despite the rapid pace of change elsewhere. Here, in this picturesque harbour town with the entrance to the port walled in by vertical rock, the narrow wooded bay, the low white houses with their green doors and the many colourful fishing boats, little has changed over the past decades, not least because the bizarre landscape doesn't allow for it. Still, new guesthouses have appeared, as well as new rows of houses in the upper streets, and everything has become more touristy. However, one thing has hardly changed at all, and that's the Bar Cala, lying immediately on the picturesque harbour.

Antonia and Lorenzo have been running this charming fish restaurant since 1957, as documented on a contemporary photograph inside. Somehow everything is as it has always been: the blue bar from the 1950s, the curved serving counter, the small turquoise mosaics, the tables set with blue-and-white cloths, the brownish pillars propping up the ceiling, the dark-blue tiles on the floor, the diffuse light. And as always, Lorenzo is sitting at one of the tables at the back, cleaning the mushrooms collected early that morning, while Antonia is filleting the fish of the day in the kitchen. And outside, on the terrace where the tables with their fine views of the harbour await, you can hear the lapping of the sea and the breaking of the waves on the rocky walls.

Cala Figuera continues to be a calm place, the lack of a sandy beach meaning an absence of tourist hubbub. Those popping into Bar Cala are mainly regulars who know that Antonia has continued to cook the same fine Mallorcan fare since she and Lorenzo moved here over half a century ago from Santanyí. Actually, one thing has changed: the restaurant has acquired a few extra storeys, allowing the couple to run a small guesthouse alongside their Bar Cala. In sleepy Cala Figuera, you need to have this additional business to survive.

Address Virgen del Carmen 56, 07659 Cala Figuera, tel. 971/645018 | Access from Santanyí via the Ma-6102; public transport: bus IB-33 from Palma via Campos and Santanyí | Opening times daily 10am–2pm and 5–10pm | Tip Spare some time to visit the Torre d'En Beu watchtower occupying a prominent position atop the cliffs on the other side of the bay.

13_The Castell de n'Amer
Strategic point on the east coast

Piracy was a cross that the Mallorcans had to bear over the centuries, with wave after wave of attacks, lootings and destruction. And it proved difficult to get rid of these sea-faring gangs. Following their raids, the pirates would quickly retreat to the other Balearic islands or to Cabrera, for instance, off Mallorca. In many cases, the pirate ships would find cover and refuge in one of the many coves along the indented coast of the island. Whichever power happened to be ruling Mallorca, the pirates developed into a permanent threat. After Ottoman pirates had plundered and almost totally destroyed the towns of Andratx, Sóller, Alcúdia and Pollença during the Turkish invasion of the Mediterranean in 1550–53, a systematic line of watchtowers was built along the coast, one after the other. In the end, more than 80 of these towers were extended into a network of fortifications.

One of them is the castle-like defensive tower of Castell de n'Amer on the protected Punta de n'Amer peninsula on the east coast of Mallorca, between Cala Millor and Sa Coma, which is covered in dunes and small pine forests. However, Castell de n'Amer, while long planned, only came into being some 100 years later following renewed attacks by North African pirates. Surrounded by a deep moat, you enter through a drawbridge. A narrow, winding stone staircase leads onto the upper artillery platform, still bearing an old cannon.

During the Spanish civil war of 1936–1939 it served as a signal and observation tower for the Francoists and was fought over heavily, temporarily falling into the hands of the Republican forces when they landed on the peninsula in 1936 in the »Battle of Mallorca«. The Castell houses a small museum with historical weapons and documents, alongside a plan detailing the fortification and watchtowers along the coast.

Address 07530 Cala Millor | Access On foot or by bike, or by car if there's not much traffic. Accessible from Sa Coma (1.5 kilometres) from the end of the northern beach promenade or from Cala Millor (1.3 kilometres) from its southern end (signposted). While the peninsula is in private hands, it it freely accessible. | Opening times daytime, free of charge | Tip The restaurant housed in a side building that once belonged to the Castell enjoys fabulous views.

14 __ The Casa March Gardens
Former residence of the island's richest man

High up on the hill above the harbour of Cala Ratjada you can spot one of the fanciest private residences on the island. Casa March is the estate of the most powerful family ever to dominate Mallorca, who for decades controlled the island's fate in every way. Alongside an ostentatious city villa in Palma and numerous other estates and lands on the island, Casa March was the seat of Juan March and his entourage, set in a voluminous landscaped park. This was the empire of Mallorca's Godfather, who piled up his billions through the most dubious of tricks, using a network of banks, shipping companies and hotels. However, to place the man in a more favourable light for future memory, the March dynasty decided to rededicate its Casa as an event space for high culture alongside an openly accessible park rich in cultural treasures. Belonging to the Fundación Bartolomé March today, the Casa remains the family's private property.

In 1915, Juan March had this opulent summer residence built on top of the ruins of a 15th-century watchtower, using ambitious architecture and fitting the interior with mosaics and wall paintings. In the 1960s, the March family had the 60-hectare park around the Villa Sa Torre Cega (»the blind tower«) lavishly designed by the renowned English landscape architect Russel Page, extending it to a sculpture garden with dozens of works by Auguste Rodin, Henry Moore and Eduardo Chillida. Inside the building, works by Picasso and Goya awaited admirers, alongside contemporary art. However, in 2001 the apocalypse broke out over Casa March. A typhoon devastated the high-lying March gardens, uprooting trees, blasting the irrigation system and demolishing numerous sculptures. Turned into a mess of rubble, the park had to be closed. It was only in mid-2011 that the gardens were ready to be reopened in their former glory, in the presence of the Spanish king.

Address Sa Torre Cega, Carrer Juan March 2, 07590 Cala Ratjada, tel. 971/563033 | Access Public transport: several buses run daily from Palma, Artà, Can Picafort and Cala Millor to Cala Ratjada (Carrer Castellet). By car, take the Ma-15 via Capdepera. | Opening times Wed–Sat by previous appointment through the tourist information on Plaça dels Pins, tel. 971/819467 | Tip Two fine and tranquil sandy beaches near Cala Ratjada, mostly left in their natural state with dune landscape and trees, are worth a visit – Cala Agulla and Cala Mesquida. The nearby Torre Embucada with its lighthouse forms the easternmost point on Mallorca.

15__ The Rock Arch

An artwork created by nature

Most holidaymakers to Mallorca reckon they know the rock arch near Cala Santanyí already. They have seen it so many times in photographs that they truly believe they've seen it with their own eyes. But this is an illusion. In fact, the gigantic rock formation off the steep cliffs at Cala Santanyí is not easy to find and difficult to access. You'll have to search out this unique place on the steep embankment, buffeted by a stiff breeze, or reach it along the cliffs beyond Cala Santanyí bay, protected from the wind by towering rocks and planted with pine trees, in the direction of the picturesque Cala Llombards.

The »Es Pontas« rock is a wonder of nature, and finding yourself in front of it takes your breath away. The sheer might and power of the stone arch jutting out of the sea simply cannot be conveyed in photographs. A massive rock formation towers over the blue waters, forming a huge free-standing bridge. This rock has been carved out by the sea for millions of years. Many call Es Pontas »Mallorca's gateway to the sea«. It goes without saying that this natural wonder is particularly popular with divers and extreme climbers.

There are numerous other exceptional rock formations, spectacular crevasses and blowholes on the island that resemble natural works of arts. In Cala de Sa Comuna, for instance, you can jump into the sea through a hole in the rock.

Just before you reach the Es Pontas rock bridge you will encounter a work of art from more recent times, but which looks no less ancient. Artist Rolf Schaffner piled up nine mighty blocks of rock to form an object six metres high, whose counterparts, according to the artist, can be found in the shape of a cross starting from Cologne, reaching up north to Trondheim, Norway, east to Volgograd in Russia, and west to Cork in Ireland. The name of this circle of objects is »Equilibrio« (Balance).

Address 07650 Cala Santanyí | Access from Santanyí via the Ma-6102; by public transport: bus IB-33 from Palma via Campos and Santanyí, just before reaching Cala Santanyí take a road leading up to the right in the direction of the Hotel Pinos Playa and park, continuing on by foot to the steep cliffs and the viewpoint | Tip The fine sandy beach in the bay of Cala Santanyí, with its steep banks, is never crowded and offers good swimming opportunities, as does the nearby Cala Llombards.

16 The Maze of Caves

A mysterious bubbling above ground

You have to duck down to avoid hitting your head on the millions-of-years-old rock formations, the steps are moist and slippery underfoot, and it would be easy to take one step too many. It is uncomfortable down here, deep in the caves of Campanet, which you walk through in a kind of subterranean posture; it's moist and warm and dimly lit, yet impressive and bizarre. Those in the know rate the maze of Campanet caves as the most beautiful and impressive of all the caves on the island. Perhaps also because there are far fewer crowds here, at the transition to the Tramuntana range, compared to the caves of Porto Cristo or Artá.

The caves of Campanet were discovered in 1945, and really rather by chance. A construction worker looking for water happened upon a hole, with air wafting up from it. The worker quickly sensed that something big was gaping there below, without initially realizing it would turn out to be a huge maze of caves dating back millions of years. The hole formed the maze's hidden access to the outer world. The owner of the grounds saw his chance and had the cave explored until 1948. The network consists of various huge halls totalling 3,200 square metres in volume and going down to 50 metres below ground. Inside the cave system you can cover some 400 metres amongst massive carbonate deposits and hundreds of stalagmite formations, some the thinnest imaginable. Above ground, another spectacular display occurs, if only a few times a year. The karst springs of Ses Fonts Ufanes are a phenomenon unique to Mallorca. In heavy rains, the ground of the holm oak forest suddenly starts bubbling, with many sources opening and the water shooting up from a subterranean reservoir. This happens three to seven times a year, between November and April, for some eight hours each time. Water pours through the forests, the brook turns into a raging torrent – until the bubbling springs dry up as quickly as they appeared.

Address 07310 Campanet, tel. 971/516130 | **Access** Ma-13 motorway Palma–Inca–Sa Pobla–Port d'Alcúdia, exit level with Sa Pobla at km 37 | **Opening times** Caves daily 10am–6pm (guided tours in English too), the springs area daily 10am–5pm | **Tip** Very close to the caves and springs, the early Gothic Capella de Sant Miquel dates back to the 13th century. One of the oldest churches on Mallorca, it boasts an impressive 16th-century altar.

17__The Ostrich Farm
South African flair on the way to Santanyí

Driving from Campos in the direction of the sea, turning onto the Ma-6014 and continuing for a few miles parallel to the coast in the direction of Ses Salines and Santanyí, you won't believe your eyes and might think you're suffering hallucinations. All of a sudden, an extensive area opens up with dozens of huge ostriches strutting about and ogling passers-by with their big eyes on long necks. A slice of southern Africa right in the heart of Mallorca.

When Uri Loffler decided to leave South Africa and move to Europe, or more specifically to Mallorca, it was to realise a long-held plan. Alongside his family he had »packed«, as it were, twelve ostriches too.

Having lived near the South African heartland of ostrich breeding, Oudtshoorn, and knowing the huge birds like the back of his hand, he had the animals shipped to Europe by container, bought some land and opened up an ostrich farm. Ostriches can reach 40 years of age or more, and two of the animals he brought over at the time are still running around happily. These formed the basis of his ostrich breeding operation.

Today the ostrich farm holds some 50 animals and the idea has become a business, family-run by the Lofflers and their two adult sons.

The farm can be visited, which is actually good fun. Kids can get really close to the animals – up to 2.5 metres high and weighing 150 kilos – by riding on them or feeding them. And on the farm anything and everything ostrich-related is used.

Son Jonathan turns the huge eggs into arty lamps, and the feathers into fancy decorations. The high-quality leather is worked into shoes and bags by Uri Loffler himself (exclusive pieces and not exactly cheap), and Mallorca's restaurants are increasingly ordering in ostrich meat.

Address Carretera Cabo Blanco, km mark 40, 07630 Campos, tel. 971/650562 or 639/721735, www.artestruzmallorca.com | Access from Campos on the Ma-6030 to Sa Ràpita, then turn left onto the Ma-6014 | Opening times daily from 8am to sunset | Tip Campos, with its 13th-century church of Sant Julián, is surrounded by well-preserved windmills waiting to be admired.

18__ The Palma Aquarium
Eye to eye with the sharks

The aquarium is a great experience for adults and children alike, on rainy days or when you've had enough of beaches, out of an interest in fish or maybe even a desire for a shot of adrenaline. »Big Blue«, over eight metres deep and holding 3.5 million litres of water, is one of the largest tanks of its kind and the aquarium's pride and joy, boasting over 1,000 fish, amongst them a dozen spectacular sharks. A panoramic tunnel allows you to move around far below the water's surface, and just as for a diver, the sharks seem close enough to touch, swimming towards you with apparently grim determination and only turning away when they have almost hit the massive glass panel.

The huge aquarium not far from the airport and near the Platja de Palma, with its large pool and play zone extending beyond the roofed-in area, was only opened in 2007, its architecture satisfying the most modern requirements.

Fifty-five different tanks contain more 8,000 marine creatures from all the oceans of the world.

The circuit through the entire aquarium, kept at a pleasant temperature by air-conditioning, making it a relief from holiday stresses on a hot summer's day, runs for just under one kilometre. The recommended visiting time is about three hours, to observe the flora and fauna not just of the Mediterranean, but also the world of the tropical seas, with their colourful fish and corals. The exhibition of living corals is well worth a visit too, not to mention the petting aquarium and the Mediterranean gardens, inspired by an Amazonian jungle, with exotic vegetation and a waterfall. There are also guided tours through the underwater world for those who fancy delving in a bit deeper, and you can enquire about feeding times at the entrance. Of course, the feeding of the sharks, taken care of by divers, is particularly fascinating.

Address Carrer Manuela de los Herreros i Sorà, 21, 07610 Palma de Mallorca (Can Pastilla), tel. 971/268382 or 902/702902, www.palmaaquarium.com | **Access** Palma-Llucmajor motorway, exit no. 10; by public transport: buses no. 15, 17, 23 from Palma stop at the door; on foot coming from the beach level with the Balneario 14 on Platja de Palma | **Opening times** April–Oct 10am–6.30pm, Jan–March 10am–4.30pm, last entry 60 minutes before closing time | **Tip** On the other side of Palma, in Costa d'en Blanes, you have the Marineland with dolphin and parrot shows.

19_ The Obelisks

Mysterious towers on the beach and in the dunes
of Can Picafort

In Can Picafort, immediately at the harbour exit, something unusual can be seen, albeit dating from more recent times. At intervals of 1,240 metres, pointed towers jut up, some ten metres high. While they have become the symbol of the town, and the coastal strip, few people know the story behind them. And not only that – these towers come with a twin another 200 metres inland. For the built-up tourist town of Can Picafort this means a tower amidst a busy junction on a crossroads.

All the obelisks between Port d'Alcúdia and Colònia de Sant Pere, most of them painted bright white with a red pointed top visible from afar, were used as orientation points for submarine captains in the Spanish Civil War and later in the Second World War. The Puntos de Referencia were also used as reference points for Spanish marines during shooting exercises as part of simulated land invasions. Submarines in particular would shoot at the target towers in the dunes.

Meanwhile the obelisks have been discovered by the Mallorcan tourism authorities and are being gradually restored.

Leaving the long, yet usually crowded beach of Can Picafort and continuing to walk along the coast, beyond the Son Bauló part of town, at the edge of a dune landscape where the rocky coast opens up, you'll encounter the prehistoric burial site of Necròpolis de Son Real boasting over 100 walled-in tombs.

Discovered in 1957, some of these above-ground necropolises from the Talayot era are situated on the small offshore island of Illa des Porros.

Covering nearly 1,000 square metres, the Son Real necropolises are considered the largest cemetery from that era (7th to 4th centuries BC) found to date on the Balearic islands.

Address Passeig de l'Enginyer Antoni Garau, 07458 Can Picafort (Santa Margalida) | **Access** Carretera Ma-12 Alcúdia – Artà level with Can Picafort | **Opening times** in summer 10am–10pm, in winter to 8pm | **Tip** The Can Picafort industrial park boasts the biggest kart racetrack in Mallorca, over one kilometre long.

20 The Crenellations

Sublime castle protecting a saint, and vice versa

The largest fortification in Mallorca is best climbed on foot, with a steep set of 150 steps leading up from the town centre. Awaiting you at the top, high up above the Capdepera rooftops, is a restored fortification, where the town dwellers once found shelter from approaching pirates. With its far-reaching views, preferably towards evening for the sunset, it makes all the climbing worthwhile.

The mountain has always attracted people. The Romans settled here to control the plain below, and the Moors extended the complex, erecting the Miquel Nunis tower between the 10th and 12th centuries. At some point the tower was converted into a mill but it is preserved to this day. In 1230, when the Moors had long since been vanquished in Palma, the Capdepera brigade were still stubbornly resisting the troops of Jaume I of Aragón and the Reconquista. Jaume II had the fort extended in around 1300, with the population living in small houses within the walls in order to protect themselves from pirate attack. For a long time, the Castell de Capdepera had a reputation for being unassailable, and it was to hold on to its function as a fortified village into the 18th century. When the town grew and acquired a new town wall, set deeper down, the castle lost its function and fell into disrepair. It took until 1983 for the restoration of this complex, the biggest of its kind on Mallorca.

Within the completely crenellated castle wall, which can be walked, the Arabic tower, the house of the governor (today containing a museum on the art of weaving palms, which were cultivated in Capdepera), and the Late Gothic chapel of the Madonna de la Esperança dating back to the 14th century, can be seen. Revered to this day, »Our Lady of Hope« is said to have repeatedly protected Capdepera from pirate attack. When she was placed atop the crenellations, it is said, thick fog would appear, making the pirates retreat. To this day, the slender Madonna has remained the patron saint of Capdepera.

Address Carrer Castell de Capdepera, 07580 Capdepera, tel. 971/818746 | Access from Palma on the Ma-15 via Manacor and Artà | Opening times 15 Oct–15 March daily 9am–5pm, 16 March–14 Oct daily 9am–8pm | Tip Near the town of Canyamel, the Coves d'Artà caves some 50 metres above the coast (in administrative terms belonging to Capdepera) are open to the public.

21 __ The Southern Tip

To the lighthouse – for its unspoilt nature

The southernmost tip of the island, it is safe to say, has its own special atmosphere. There is no bus connection, few tour coaches find their way here, and you won't even encounter that many cars. Those who do drive or hike into this slice of near-untouched landscape are people who can't get enough of bizarre-looking nature, who like their peace and quiet and want to escape completely the hustle and bustle of the beaches. There's not much here apart from landscape and nature, not even any gastronomy. On fine days you get views reaching all the way to Cabrera Island, and of course you'll see the white lighthouse with its elongated keeper's house marking Mallorca's southernmost point, an attraction not only for lighthouse lovers. Often though, the Cap is shrouded in storm clouds, with waves several metres high whipping the rocky coast and scattering the spray. After just a few minutes here the skin starts tasting salty.

On the drive to the Cap de Ses Salines you'll pass the saltworks of Sa Vall, alongside those at Colònia Sant Jordi some of the oldest on the island, which were used in Roman times for salt extraction through the evaporation of seawater. Other than that, most of the southern tip of Mallorca belongs to the March family of bankers – i.e. in private hands and largely, such as the S'Avall country estate, fenced off. However, don't let that spoil your fun.

Choose a fine day to hike down the coast from the lighthouse, best in the direction of Colònia de Sant Jordi and always hugging the cliffs. You'll discover many fascinating bird species as, alongside the native birds, thousands of migratory birds land here on their way from Africa to their nesting places in Europe. There are no swimming options near the lighthouse, but carry on walking for half an hour, albeit through fairly inhospitable terrain, to encounter the Platja des Caragol, a slice of true solitude far from any tourism, as this beach is only accessible on foot.

Address Cap de Ses Salines (belonging to the municipality 07650 Santanyí) | **Access** from Palma take the Ma-19 to Llucmajor, Campos and Santanyí, from there, or from Ses Salines on the Ma-6100 and Ma-6110 to the lighthouse at the Cap de Ses Salines | **Tip** In Ses Salines, take a look at the Sant Bartomeu church (1876) and the ruins of the 13th-century Torre de Can Bárbara fort.

22 __ The Talayot Settlement

Touch prehistory and marvel

Capocorb Vell is probably the most important prehistoric settlement on Mallorca, or in any case the one that is best preserved, despite the efforts of the 13th-century Christian re-conquerors under King Jaume I, who in their anger at anything foreign had parts of the ancient Talayot settlement and surrounding wall torn down to use the large blocks for building new churches, the cathedral in Palma in particular.

However, to this day there is still plenty to see in Capocorb Vell. The ruins probably date from the 12th century BC, making them the oldest traces of human settlement on Mallorca. The Bronze Age Talayot culture lasted between 1400 and 1000 BC. Some 500 people probably lived here, not far from Llucmajor, in megalithic dwellings built using a dry-stone technique where the stones were hewn into square shapes and then layered on top and into each other. This megalithic architecture, in use on the Balearics up to the Roman era, can be found across the entire Mediterranean.

What you see today, on an excavated surface of some 7,000 square metres, are five relatively well-preserved talayots – three round fortified towers up to six metres high with extremely thick walls and two square talayots – some of which are two-storied with a stone floor, plus two dozen living units, all surrounded by the remains of a defensive wall. It is presumed that Capocorb Vell was inhabited from the Bronze Age into the early Middle Ages, but archaeologists have no definitive answers to questions of the true character of Talayot culture and these buildings.

Were they actual defensive structures, sites of ritual sacrifice, or mainly living spaces? Mallorca is said to have held up to 200 villages of this kind. Alongside Capocorp Vell, the settlements of Ses Païsses near Artà, Necrópolis near Can Picafort and Son Fornés near Montuiri have also survived.

Address Poblado Talayótico de Capocorb Vell, 07620 Llucmajor, tel. 971/180155 | Access
Ma-19 Palma in the direction Llucmajor, exit km 26, Ma-6015 in the direction of S'Estanyol,
at km 11 turn off onto the Ma-6014 in the direction of Cala Pi to km 23 | Opening times
daily 10am–5pm, closed on Thu | Tip The Museum Arqueológico Son Fornés in Monturi
gives hands-on insights into the Talayot culture and megalithic architecture.

23__ The Cabrera Visitor Centre

An archipelago of scenic beauty and fertile history

Romantic souls think of the island of Cabrera, off the southernmost tip of Mallorca, as a slice of near-untouched nature, while historians know it as the merciless old prison island which in the early years of the 19th century became the »Hell of Cabrera«. The Spanish War of Independence (1808–1814) was raging, when Spain rose up against the Napoleonic troops seeking domination over the Iberian peninsula. When the Spanish were able to inflict a devastating defeat on the French at the Battle of Bailén in 1808, taking some 18,000 prisoners, they shipped about 9,000 of them onto the almost uninhabited island of Cabrera. The prisoners were interned in the old fortification which had been built in the 14th century to ward off pirates and smugglers.

For the most part, the soldiers were left to their own devices, forgotten by the rest of the world. There was barely enough food, insufficient water and no medical care. Some 6,000 French soldiers died in this six-year imprisonment, suffering hunger, disease and epidemics. To this day, inscriptions on the walls of the fortification remain as silent testimonies to the human drama played out during those years.

Situated just under 14 kilometres off the coast, the Cabrera archipelago, with its 17 small rocky islets and the main island, is known to only a few Mallorcans, even though the military fortification and garrison island was declared a national park in 1991. You'll find just a few houses and military barracks and a handful of inhabitants, but the archipelago's biodiversity more than makes up for this. Remember that no more than 200 visitors are allowed onto the island each day. Opened in 2008, the Cabrera Visitor Centre in Colònia de Sant Jordi takes its architectural inspiration from a Talayot and is well worth visiting.

Address Visitor Centre of the Cabrera national park, Carrer Gabriel Roca 20, 07638 Colònia de Sant Jordi, tel. 971/656282 | Access By boat from Colònia de Sant Jordi between April and Oct daily (except during stormy seas) at 9.30am, returning around 5pm. Driving time one hour. Take a picnic as there are no cafes. Visiting the island unaccompanied is not permitted. Bookings for ferry boats at the port, tel. 971/649034. | Opening times daily 10am–2.30pm and 3.30–6pm | Tip A visit to the Blue Grotto of Sa Cova Blava in Cabrera, only accessible from the sea, is a must. The play of the light is unbelievable, swimming is permitted and the whole thing is a true experience.

24__ The Planetarium

A clear view of the skies at the island's centre

Of course you can use Mallorca's good weather, its azure-blue sky, the dry air and clear views to lie in the sun and get a tan. Or you could use the wonderful Mediterranean sky to get up close and personal with the stars above Mallorca. The best way to do this is a visit to the island's modern planetarium, which opened in 2004 and boasts spectacular architecture. You will find it near the small settlement of Costitx, aligned exactly in the centre of the island, immediately next to the Observatorio Astrónomico de Mallorca, which has been here since 1991 and also runs the planetarium.

Conditions are excellent here in Costitx, in the vicinity of this community of 1,000 inhabitants, with no high mountains, no surprising changes in the weather and no influences from the sea. This is an invitation to use your time on Mallorca to take a trip to the solar system and faraway planets, leaving sun, beach and palms behind for a few hours.

In the observatory, the dome opens to let you look deep into the sky by telescope. Next door, at the touch of a button, the state-of-the-art planetarium projector Skymaster ZKP4, developed by Zeiss, beams 6,000 stars onto the 360-degree surround screen below a 14-metre metal dome, with 110 visitors able to follow the show. The images are sent in by supercomputer from the world's most important telescopes, in real time and in extra-high definition. This is something you won't find anywhere else in Europe. Of course visitors may also use telescopes to simply look into the real-life sky above Mallorca.

Over the past few years, the observatory, the Balearics' only astronomy centre whose main objective is contributing to science, has time and again found hitherto unknown objects. One of the last stars discovered from Costitx was named after Mallorcan tennis player Rafael Nadal.

Address Camí de l'Observatori, 07144 Costitx, tel. 971/513344 or mobile 649/997752, www.mallorcaplanetarium.com | Access Ma-3240 Carretera Inca–Sineu, exit Costitx at km 7, from Costitx follow the minor road to Sencelles, exit at Parc Verd and follow the signs | Opening times Tue–Sun 8pm, groups by appointment; for night sessions in the observatory, reservations and information Mon–Fri 9.30am–1.30pm, tel. 650/386881 | Tip The remains of a temple from the Talayot culture stand near the Son Corró estate on the road to Sencelles. In 1894, three bulls' heads were discovered here, dating back to the 6th century BC.

25_ The Carrara Temple

The backdrop to an Austrian archduke's meditations

What an estate, this Son Marroig, what an incomparably privileged location. And what an eccentric owner this Austrian archduke, Ludwig Salvatore (1847–1915) must have been. Having this old fortified finca with its defensive tower high above the Costa Nord redesigned in the Italian style, he filled it with the kind of life you can only guess at when you enter and take a wander there today, even though it was turned into a museum as far back as 1928. You can easily imagine this maverick, who enjoyed a liberal education – with plenty of natural history – and material independence and who escaped the narrow norms of the Viennese court, sitting below the round canopy of the little pavilion built from Italian Carrara marble, inspired by antiquity, and getting drunk on the view. Ludwig would share this experience with friends, guests and lovers, and twice too with his cousin, Empress Elizabeth, known affectionately as Sissi, who visited him here. Their playground was the wide sea, the enchanted path down to the cove that sheltered his steam-yacht Nixe, which he used to explore every last nook and cranny of the Mediterranean, and the rocky isthmus of Na Foradada 250 metres below the estate, resembling a natural wonder with its 18-metre hole in the rocky wall.

The archduke had purchased land from the farmers between Valldemossa and Deià that stretched for miles along the coast and deep into the countryside. Alongside the old derelict monastery of Miramar he added the Son Marroig estate in 1872 and was to live there after its conversion until 1913. He had paths cut and viewpoints made accessible to anybody. He banned the felling of trees or any kind of hunting on his estate. Ludwig Salvatore was a patron of the noblest kind. A fluent speaker of Mallorcan who always remained close to the people and is revered on the island to this day, he wrote a number of books, amongst them »The Balearic Islands«, which runs to several illustrated volumes.

Address Carretera Valldemossa–Sóller, 07179 Deià | Access Ma-10 between Deià and Valldemossa, turning off at km 65.5 to the carpark, bus L 210 from Palma via Valldemossa | Opening times April–Sept Mon–Sat 9.30am–7.30pm, Oct–March 9.30am–5.30pm, closed Sun | Tip Very close by, the Monestir de Miramar monastery, founded by King Jaume II in 1276 and restored by the archduke in 1872, boasts fine cloisters.

26__ The Writer's Grave

Robert Graves' resting place in the mountains

From the 1920s onwards, the small village of Deià in the Tramuntana mountain range enjoyed a reputation as a haven for artists. Painters, musicians and most of all writers settled here, inspired by the beauty of the landscape, the mild climate and the flair of the place, with the Cala Deià beach nearby. This image remained well into the 1980s, with legendary artists' meetings and roaring parties in the houses and bars. Deià has kept a lot of its atmosphere today. The place has not been built up too much and has remained authentic, just a bit more chic perhaps, with fewer resident artists. Still, Deià continues to breathe these spiritual origins and in no way lives off its past, when writers such as Jakov Lind and Robert Graves would dominate the place. Graves (1895–1985), in particular, lived here from the 1940s and left his mark on this little village, making it an international celebrity.

Thus it came about that the author of »I, Claudius« was buried in the small cemetery next to the parish church of Sant Joan, high up on the hill and accessible through narrow lanes. The house, Ca N'Alluny, where Graves spent over half a century, was turned into a museum in 2006 and gives an idea of the writer's life and work.

In fact, it was Graves' fame that attracted an increasing number of artists to Deià. Of the writers and painters he invited to stay, many went on to settle here. In the 1960s and 70s numerous bohemians and hippies joined the throng, and the picturesque village with its olive terraces and citrus fruit at the foot of the Berges Teix mountain, over 1,000 metres high, became ever more colourful and creative. Ava Gardner lived here, as well as Peter Ustinov, the iconic Austrian-French reporter Georg Stefan Troller, and Andrew Lloyd Webber. Today, Deià still cultivates the image of an artists' colony, and in truth a number of artistic folk work, exhibit, sell and live here, even though a new set of wealthy incomers have increasingly come to dominate the village.

Address Plaça des Puig, 07179 Deià | **Access** Ma-10 if coming in from Sóller or Vallde-mossa; by public transport: bus L 210 Palma–Valldemossa–Deià–Sóller | **Opening times** Museum Tue–Sat 10am–5pm, in winter to 4pm | **Tip** Take a look at the tiny village of Lluc Alcari just a few miles beyond Deià in the direction of Sóller. The Cala de Deià is one of the most beautiful coves for swimming along the Tramuntana coast, and the Hotel Residencia with its restaurant El Olivio ranks amongst Mallorca's top hospitality spots.

27__ The Table Mountain
High place of refuge for the nobility

Did you know that Mallorca has its own table mountain? While it doesn't quite have the might of its larger cousin in South Africa's Cape Town, it makes a decent miniature version. Coming towards it from the south, it suddenly emerges as a slightly confusing presence in the landscape. From below you can already make out the contours of the ruined Castell de Santueri, and driving up to it is a true experience. While the road is narrow and uneven, and hence little-used, the landscape on either side, with its palm and cypress, almond and orange trees, is a sight for sore eyes. And what awaits you at the edge of the 400-metre-high plateau is a slice of Roman, Arabic – and later on, Spanish history too – that you can delve into, as time has stood still up here. For centuries, next to nothing was changed in the architecture of the mighty fortifications, which consist mostly of a ruined castle. This is usually closed for safety reasons, so you'll only get as far as the gate, but this makes no dent on the overwhelming impression.

The old masters of the castle would certainly have seen their enemies coming from afar. At the time of the Romans, around 100 BC, the castle already had a fortified tower, and after the conquest by the Arabs a proper fortification was erected here. During the Reconquista Jaume I conquered the Castell following an intense siege, and razed it almost completely. From the 14th century onwards the castle was rebuilt mainly as a refuge from the constantly increasing pirate attacks. In the 1520s it then served as a place of refuge for the landed gentry during the bloody revolts of the craftsmen's guilds and the rural population against the oppressive tax burden, which became known as the Germania revolt. Since the 18th century the castle has been left to nature, slowly becoming overgrown. Today the entire complex is supposed to be fully restored and the table mountain made accessible to the public – a rewarding project for a historical monument in a superb location.

Address Castell de Santueri, 07200 Felanitx | Access from Felanitx on the Ma-4010 in the direction of Portocolom or on the Ma-14 to Santanyí | Opening times The entrance gate is only open occasionally; should you find it closed, ask for the key at the Sa Possecio d'es Castell farm at the foot of the hill. | Tip In Felanitx don't miss the Sant Miquel church above the Plaça d'Espanya, with its mighty free-standing staircase and Stations of the Cross leading to Calvary, and the windmills on the eastern hills of the town.

28_ The Lighthouse at the Cap

It's the end of the island as we know it

To get from Port de Pollença to Cap de Formentor at the very tip of the long peninsula in the far north of Mallorca, you're looking at another 20 kilometres of road. And it's the kind of road that can take a lot out of a driver. Full of twists and turns, its hairpin bends require maximum concentration, and in season it is full of cars. However, the views awaiting you along this stretch more than make up for the effort. They range from the Mirador de Mal Pas high above the sea, to the little rocky offshore islet of Fe Colomer far below, and for particularly hardened drivers there is the 16th-century pirate's tower of Talaia d'Albercutx even higher up. Not for the faint-hearted, up here the rock walls drop 300 metres, while the wind rages and deep below the sea whips itself into a frenzy.

And then, after a few more miles and a few more bends you've reached the tip of the peninsula, Cap de Formentor with its white lighthouse visible from afar at the furthermost end of the massive rocks, over 200 metres above the water and pushing out far into the blue sea. The Faro de Formentor lighthouse was built in 1892, while its beacon, with a reach of over 60 kilometres, is considered the strongest of all the lighthouses on the Balearics.

For a long time, Formentor belonged to the family of Mallorcan poet Miquel Costa i Llobera, who spent many years of his life on the peninsula. Following his death in 1922 the hotel was sold. One of the buyers, in 1928, was an Argentinian who built the legendary Hotel Formentor on the edge of Platja de Formentor, and would always welcome European VIPs from the political world and film business. Today, the five-star hotel belongs to the Barceló group. Also in the 1920s, the Italian engineer Antonio Parietti designed and built the winding road in this surreal landscape, opening up Formentor to new visitors, which earned him a monument at the Mirador de Mas Pas.

Address Carrer de Formentor, 07470 Port de Pollença | **Access** From Port de Pollença on the Ma-2210 Carrer de Formentor. By public transport: there are buses leaving from Port de Pollença and Port d'Alcúdia. In Port de Pollença you can also book a boat trip to Cap de Formentor. | **Tip** A recommended stop for a dip is Platja de Formentor or the hidden cove of Cala Figuera on the peninsula's northern side, accessible on foot from a car park.

29__ The Camper Shop

Leather and shoes from Inca are still in demand

Shops selling shoes and leather goods are everywhere in Inca. Shoes have been produced here since the Middle Ages, turning into an industry at the end of the 19th century. Inca then gained a reputation as a leather town which reached far beyond Mallorca. Lottusse, Barrats, Farrutx, Kollflex and Camper are the most prominent brands for leather goods, of which Camper is probably the best known internationally. The family behind the name Camper – the company of that name was only founded in the mid-1970s – is the Fluxà family, boasting a tradition that stretches back over 130 years.

In 1877 the accomplished shoemaker Antonio Fluxà travelled from Inca to England, to familiarise himself with the latest methods of industrial shoe production. He introduced those new methods of manufacturing shoes to Inca, and his son would go on to create ever more product lines. Historically already a centre of shoe and leather manufacturing, Mallorca's economy now gained a second industrial pillar, alongside tourism and agriculture. As the fourth generation of the Fluxà family began to use environmentally-friendly production methods to create a trend around the traditionally light shoes worn on the island, Camper shoes became bestsellers. The name »Camper«, derived from the Mallorcan »els campers«, the peasants, became synonymous with a comfortable, extremely light and ecologically sustainable shoe. In 1981, the first Camper shop opened in Barcelona, followed ten years later by the brand's international expansion.

Today, you can also buy shoes direct from Camper in the Polígono industrial zone on the edge of Inca, seat of the headquarters and design studio, even though most of them are now manufactured abroad where they are cheaper to produce. And those wanting to delve deeper into Mallorca's leather and shoe industry should pay a visit to the newly-opened leather museum, Museu del Calzado, on Avinguda General Luque.

Address Re-Camper Shop, Poligono Industrial s/n, 07300 Inca, tel. 971/888233 | **Access** Inca enjoys a central location and is easily accessible by bus or train. The shoe factories are situated on the Ma-13a ringroad in the direction of Palma. | **Opening times** in summer Mon–Sat 10am–8.30pm, at other times Mon–Sat 10am–8pm | **Tip** Don't forget to try out one of the numerous cosy cellars in the town centre, old underground pubs that used to be wine cellars and today offer excellent Mallorcan fare. On Thursdays, Inca has a large market, again offering an endless supply of leather goods. Kollflex in nearby Selva still allow visitors to take a look inside the production workshop.

30__The Blue Children's Choir

The famous choir of Lluc monastery

The whole thing seems rather spooky. Some 40 young boys in blue-and-white gowns suddenly appear in front of the Black Madonna, move into line as if by magic and start singing like angels. After two hymns, not even ten minutes long, they disappear again the way they came. This ritual takes place several times a week at 11.15 on the dot in the Basilica des Santuari de Lluc, leaving an impression that lasts long after they've gone. Ave Maria de Lluc.

»Els Blauets« is the name of the singing marvels, »the Blue Ones«. And hardly anyone knows that this is one of the oldest choirs in Europe. In 1526, the then prior of the monastery decided that some boys should sing regularly as part of early Mass. A few years later, this tradition turned into a choir and the ritual of the daily performance of the »Salve Regina« was born, a celebration of Mallorca that is a firm part of the spirituality surrounding the »Moreneta«, or Black Madonna, which is revered on the island like no other statue. On Mallorca, the Lluc monastery is the centre of Marian worship and the most important pilgrimage site.

All the boys, and of late a few girls too, are pupils at one of the most renowned schools in Mallorca, the Escolania de Lluc, a monastic boarding school, which has been in existence since 1532. This is where the young people live and receive their entire schooling, alongside an intensive musical education. Between 40 and 50 »Blauets« are active in the choir. And because of the blue collars and sleeves, the blue frocks and white shirts of their cassocks, they still bear that name, »the Blue Ones«. The choir always performs in this garb, even for guest performances outside the monastery in various churches and cathedrals of European cities, London's Westminster Abbey for instance.

El mes de

novembre

tots som

EDALLA

D'OR DEL

ONSERVATORI

PENJA-TE-LA !!

Address 07315 Santuari de Lluc, tel. 971/871525 | Access from Inca on the Ma-2130 |
Opening times The monastery and basilica remain open all day. The choir performs daily
at 11.15am and during Sunday Mass. | Tip Don't miss the botanical gardens behind the
monastery.

31__ The Aubocassa Olive Plantation

The island gold grows on trees

The story of the Aubocassa country estate goes back to the 12th century, and when you reach it – a few miles beyond Manacor on a small country road – it feels like entering a film set. This stately-looking old property, with its own little church, is framed by cypress trees and surrounded by extensive olive groves. Today, the estate belongs to the Bodegas Roda, who are now based on the Spanish mainland in Haro (La Rioja) but have set up their own satellite operation here. The cultivation of olives has been a central part of Mallorca for centuries, and the vineyards of Aubocassa produce them on a large scale. The plantation comprises around 8000 olive trees, of the Arbequína variety, over an area of 24 hectares. For one litre of olive oil you need eight kilos of olives, and every year 60,000 bottles are produced here, of which some 80 per cent are consumed in Spain.

Olive trees form part of the image we have of the island, along with wind and watermills, only more timeless. Apparently it was the Phoenicians who, a good 3000 years ago, brought the first olive trees to Mallorca. Since then these bizarre figures have paid silent testimony to entire historical eras. Many olive trees are up to 500, even 1000 years old in some cases. Those used for producing oil are of course younger and provide a higher yield. In any case, they grow well in the Mediterranean climate, are resistant against wind, weather and pests, and every year they bear the secret gold of the island: olives. In many different flavours and varieties too. Olive trees have been used systematically for agriculture since the 16th century. The olives are harvested as fresh as possible, ideally in November. Just a few hours after picking they are processed through so-called cold centrifugation, meaning with no subsequent filtering. Aubocassa is the place to find out about olive oil production.

Address Camí de Son Fangos, km 7, 07500 Manacor, tel. 670/846622 and 679/516863 | **Access** Coming from Palma on the Ma-15 to Manacor, then at the exit of the village turn into Camì de Son Fangos until you reach km 7. | **Opening times** Mon–Fri 9am–1pm and 3–5pm. The olive plantation may be visited by individuals and groups of up to 20 people, just phone ahead to book. | **Tip** One of Mallorca's best olive oils is produced by the Solivellas family on their country estate of Es Guinyent near Alcúdia (tel. 971/545722). Another centre of olive oil production is Sóller.

32__ The City of Artificial Pearls
Shopping around for the best imitation

Of course this is all a bit touristy, but you should see it anyway, just once. Artificial pearls happen to form part of Mallorcan island culture and industrial history in equal measure, and Mallorca's second-largest city, Manacor, is its centre.

The most important company, which turned Manacor into the city of artificial pearls and gave »Mallorca Pearls« their name, is the Majorica firm, to this day the most important producer of imitation pearls.

Majorica goes back to German entrepreneur Eduard Friedrich Hugo Heusch (1865–1937), who in 1902 turned his idea of large-scale artificial pearl production into reality in Manacor. The same gentleman secured the patent for this kind of manufacture of artificial pearls, which are difficult to tell apart from the real mother-of-pearl thing even by experts in the field. It was a well-kept company secret of Majorica's, even though in 1948, as the patent expired and with it the monopoly of the Heusch family, a number of rivals joined the pearly lineup. Today, Majorica is a listed company in the hands of various groups of investors.

Production of the Mallorca pearls has remained the same over the decades, although some are produced by machine now too. The procedure is complex and labour-intensive. The pearls are manufactured around a hardened synthetic core before being dipped into a blend of fish scales and shell sand, heated and dried repeatedly. Added colourful minerals give hues of colour. Once all the layers have been applied and hardened, the pearls are cut and polished. Imitation pearls from Manacor are a brand known all over the world, not least for their long durability and visual authenticity, and are often used by manufacturers of intricate pearl jewellery. The factory salesroom provides an impressive demonstration of pearl manufacture by various skilled workers.

Address Perlas Majorica, Via Roma 48, 07500 Manacor, tel. 971/550200 | Access By public transport: buses several times a day from Palma, Inca, Porto Cristo, Cala Millor and Cala Ratjada, as well as the train from Palma via Inca; by car: coming from Palma take the Ma-15, exit km 47 | Opening times Show production: Mon–Fri 9am–1pm and 2.30–7pm; sale: Mon–Fri 9am–8pm, Sat, Sun 9.30am–1pm | Tip Driving towards the sea from Manacor you will hit the Coves dels Hams and the Coves del Drac, or dragon's den, with its subterranean Lake Martel.

33__ The Trotting Track
»Trot« in Manacor and Palma

Trotting races are very popular in Mallorca, and on race days Mallorcans mingle at the track in Palma or Manacor. A visit to one of the two racecourses is worth it if only to experience the authentic Mallorca. And you don't have to be a horse lover or gambler. Trotting is a way of life on Mallorca, and there are more horse owners than you might think, preparing their horses back on the finca to be pitted against their rivals at weekends, the winner pocketing several hundred euros.

Trotting or harness racing, called »trot« on Mallorca, has some 30,000 aficionados and is second only to football in terms of sporting popularity on the island. A purely Balearic sport, being entirely unknown on the Spanish mainland, trotting emerged from the cart races held at the end of big market days.

The breeders of the »trotons«, those specifically Balearic bred, of which there are roughly 6000, are extremely passionate about what they do. In the east of the island in particular, around Manacor, you'll find numerous stables. Training takes place on small courses around the fincas and during the week on the racetracks of Manacor and Palma.

The trotting track in Manacor was built in 1929 and has been modernised several times since, today being equipped with computers and an electronic betting system.

At its centre you'll see a grandstand, with some seats behind glass, across three storeys. Betting is a big factor of course, but the value of these weekend events – floodlit in winter – is not to be underestimated.

The most important and prestigious race of the year, with the highest stakes, is the Gran Premio Nacional held at the trotting course in Palma on the third weekend in May. The only horses allowed to start here are three-year olds born in Spain.

Address Hipòdrom de Manacor, 07500 Manacor, tel. 971 / 823492 | Access on the Palma–Artà road, km 48 | Opening times Events take place on a Saturday or Sunday, with racing usually starting at 4pm. | Tip Another trotting track is the Hipòdrom Son Pardo in Palma. For information on the next racing events on Mallorca contact the Federación Balear de Trote, Carretera de Sóller, km 3.5 (Hipòdrom Son Pardo), 07009 Palma, tel. 971 / 468508 or 661 / 862669, office hours Mon–Fri 8am–3pm, www.federaciobaleardetrot.com.

34 The Plaça de Toros
Bullfighting is set to continue here

Seemingly deaf to the protests provoked all over the island these days by the bloody spectacle, the town of Muro is planning to uphold the tradition of the corrida by continuing to stage bullfights. Bullfighting not only repels most tourists, but also an increasing number of Mallorcans, headed of course by the local animal rights campaigners and, above all, by young people. The debate around the pros and cons of corridas was particularly intensified by the legally binding ban on bullfights in Catalunya, which took effect in 2011. There are vehement demands for its extension to the Balearics too. However, the autonomous region of Mallorca is not willing to bow to external pressure and looks set to hold on to this Spanish tradition for the time being.

Bullfight or no bullfight, for the »mureros«, the inhabitants of Muro, their bullfighting arena is sacred. And now, as ever, they await feverishly the annual corrida on 24 June, the day of their patron saint San Joan Baptiste. Tickets for the »La Monumental« arena, seating 6,000 spectators, and the traditional six fights with three toreros, always sell out in a flash. Since the influential citizen Jaime Serra Palau decided around 1920 to build a bullfighting ring here, this day is one of the highlights of a town otherwise not exactly rich in events. And he didn't just build any old bullring – the arena was to rise from a large stone quarry. It took several years to drill the circular amphitheatre with its diametre of 37.5 metres and seats hewn laboriously out of the rock. There is nothing in all of Spain to compare to an arena such as »La Monumental« in Muro. And Spanish bullfighters hold the »Monumental de Muro« dear as a place where you have to have fought at least once in your life. In 2010, the Muro bullring was bought by the town hall from private hands for half a million euros. Today, it presents its splendour anew in defiance of the winds of change.

Address La Monumental, Plaça de Toros, 07440 Muro, tel. 971/860826 | Access from Manacor via Santa Margalida, from Palma via Inca and Sa Pobla | Opening times Event information is available, but the arena may be seen from outside too. | Tip Alongside the »La Monumental« in Muro, built around 1920, there is the Coliseo Balear in Palma (1929), the Plaça de Toros de Alcúdia (1892), the La Macarena in Felanitx (1914) and the Plaça de Toros in Inca (1910), which has housed the Museo Taurino bullfighting museum since 2008. The Museu Etnòlogic de Muro is particularly recommended.

35__ The Arabic Baths
Moorish relic in the Old Town garden

This is a place to discover the kind of Moorish architecture that left its mark on Palma, and Mallorca in general, for three centuries up to the Reconquista. Few tourists find their way into the Arabic Baths, of which Palma once had five. Yet this monument to the island's cultural history is a must-see for anyone wanting more from their holiday than just beach and sun. A great attraction of the place is that here, just behind the cathedral, you can completely relax, sometimes on your own, between the lemon trees, cacti and palm trees in the gardens of the Can Fontirroig manor house surrounding the Banys Arabs. The entire complex probably used to be part of a palace or a Moorish castle.

Dating back to the 11th century, the baths, or rather what is left of them after they were used as stables up to the 1960s, once belonged to an Arabic nobleman, when Palma still went by the name of Medina Mayurqa.

The baths consist of two buildings. The larger of the two halls, built in the Roman style, is the caldarium, where hot steam baths took place. The vault, its dome clad in shimmering red stone, is supported by twelve narrow pillars. Small circular openings in the semi-circular ceiling of the dome would let steam escape. As the pillars all have different capitals, art historians presume that the Arabs had them taken from old Roman buildings in their sphere of influence and shipped to Palma.

The steam bath also had a two-layered marble floor, which acted as a kind of under-floor heating as the space between the layers would heat from the cauldrons of the domestic rooms and kitchen quarters below. The second room, the tepidarium, with a cross vault and whose original rich decorations can only be guessed at today, was a warm space and considered an ante-room before entering the caldarium.

Address Can Serra 7, 07001 Palma de Mallorca, tel. 971/721549 | **Access** a few metres behind the cathedral, past the Museu Diocesà via the Passeig de Dalt Murada into Can Serra | **Opening times** April–Nov 9am–7.30pm, Dec–March 9am–6pm | **Tip** A few steps from the Arabic Baths, the Palau Aiamans Renaissance palace shelters the Museo de Mallorca (Carrer de la Portella 5) with the most comprehensive historic collection on the island – from the Talayot culture to 20th century art.

36 __ The Arms Museum
Calm amid the arms

Twice a year, the Queen Mary 2 is welcomed to the port of Palma. When that happens, the world's largest cruiseship seems to fill the Porto Pi terminal to bursting point.

In season however, »regular« cruiseships form part of the daily life of this part of Palma. Above the mooring places of cruisers and ocean liners, the time-honoured Castell de Sant Carles (1610) on the peninsula, once the fortification of Porto Pi, holds the island's arms and military museum.

For those interested in Spanish history, and Mallorcan history in particular, this museum, opened in 1981, is a treat – despite the many weapons and a history full of armed conflict. There are fabulous views across the Bay of Palma from the roof of the completely restored Castell, amidst numerous historic howitzers and cannons giving you an idea of how enemy ships were greeted from this defensive position. Until 1980, the castle was used as an artillery barracks and military prison.

Today, the visitor is greeted by numerous rooms inside the fortification, the visit starting from the courtyard below the tall watchtower. The collection of war artefacts and military equipment spans the Middle Ages to the 20th century, but holds some older pieces too from the time of the Knights Templar and the Reconquista. The miniature battlefield with hundreds of figures representing Hannibal's army is impressive.

Even if military memorabilia is not your thing you'll enjoy the visit, as despite all the armaments, the castle exudes an immense calm and everything is far less menacing than you might think.

There is always a fresh breeze blowing up here at this elevation, and the café under pine trees is a cosy place for a rest. The museum courtyard often puts on classical concerts, which are musical highlights of Palma's cultural calendar.

Address Museu Històric Militar de les Balears, Castell de Sant Carles, Carrer Dock West, Dic de l'Oest, 07015 Palma de Mallorca, Porto Pi, tel. 971/402145 | Access Public transport: bus no. 1, stop Dic d l'Oest (last stop) | Opening times Mon–Fri 9am–1pm, Sat 10am–1pm | Tip Make sure you take a stroll along the harbour walk with its fishing port, the royal yacht club and the marina. Boat trips around the harbour or for the day are also on offer here.

37__The Arts Cinema

*Films and much more entertainment
in the former abattoir*

The speciality of this cinema, unique in Palma, is to show international films in the original version. This of course is music to the ears of the English- or German-speaking residents, but also to those visitors to Palma who fancy taking in a good film alongside all the tourist activities.

With its four small dedicated screens, the Cine Ciutat (form. »Renoir«) is the only arts cinema in Palma, which doesn't mean however that only heavy stuff is shown. On the contrary, you can see all the best current films, in the original with Spanish subtitles. There are also films synchronised into English, so you don't have to forego cinematic pleasures in Palma even if you don't speak Spanish or Catalan.

The Cine Ciutat forms part of the S'Escorxador information and arts centre, which has become ever more popular over the past few years and is housed in Palma's former abattoir.

When the municipal abattoir S'Escorxador Municipal was built in 1904 by architect Gaspar Bennassar i Moner, it was outside the city along the road to Valldemossa. Considered a great architectural success and winner of various prizes, the different parts of the building were functionally laid out around a patio, built from limestone and augmented with numerous iron constructions and projecting glass roofs.

Once the abattoir closed in 1982, the imposing buildings fell into disrepair before being renovated and restored thoroughly in 1990. The renovation works retained the former abattoir's characteristic architecture, its red facade and high-ceilinged rooms.

Today, the building next to the Cine Ciutat houses a library, various cafés and a beer garden, which is becoming ever more popular amongst the good people of Palma.

Address Cine Ciutat, Carrer Emperadriu Eugènia 6, 07010 Palma de Mallorca, tel. 971/
297301 | Access by car: from Plaça d'Espanya via Joan March and Comte de Sallent into
Carrer Blanquerna in the direction of Valldemossa, taking a right at its end | Opening times
Screening times can be found in the daily newspapers or on sites such as , otherwise the
S'Escorxador is open around the clock. | Tip If you're looking for a complete contrast to
arthouse cinema, head for the Salas Ocimax, Palma's largest cinema, with 14 screens, digital
surround sound and 3-D technology (Carrer Bisbe Pere Puigdorfila, on the Ma-20 near
Carretera Valldemossa).

38__ The Barceló Chapel

Modern Art in Palma's venerable Cathedral

When the Spanish royal couple visited Palma Cathedral in February 2007, they brought a large delegation of Catalan dignitaries and artists with them. The cathedral, which has sat high above the Old Town for the past 700 years and ranks amongst the very best examples of sacred Gothic architecture in Spain or even Europe, saw the inauguration of a very unusual work of art: an enormous ceramic piece by Mallorcan artist Miquel Barceló. This gave Palma one more attraction, although many visitors don't find this contemporary work of art easy to comprehend.

Born in 1957 in Felanitx, Miquel Barceló had been commissioned in 2000 by the former bishop of Palma, Teodoro Úbeda, to design a motif from the New Testament for the chapel dedicated to Saint Peter (Capella de Sant Pere) at the end of the cathedral's right-hand lateral nave. This commission for a contemporary abstract artwork in the venerable cathedral was even more surprising, as Barceló has a reputation as a critic of religion. The result was a wall tableau made from clay and ceramics covering 300 square metres, across almost the entire chapel. It represents the Biblical story telling of the miraculous »multiplication of the loaves and fishes« during the feeding of the five thousand.

The imposing wall relief, 16 metres tall, shows a sketched figure of Christ flanked by everything the sea has to offer: waves and swell with fish coming to the surface for air, as well as loaves of bread and shoals of fish. The five stained-glass windows, also designed by Barceló in dark blues and greys, represent the depths of the sea. The artist created a work of art that seems to come from the very core of the island. Still, it remains controversial, as did the work by his famous predecessor Antoni Gaudí, who redesigned the cathedral at the beginning of the 20th century and whose artistry is such a firm part of the building now.

Address Catedral de la Seu, Plaça Almoina, 07001 Palma de Mallorca | Access on foot, up
the steps from Passeig de Born | Opening times April–May, Oct Mon–Fri 10am–5.15pm,
June–Sept Mon–Fri 10am–6.15pm, Nov–March 10am–5.15pm, all year round
Sat 10am–2.15pm | Tip The walls of the Royal Chapel with its glass ceramics were designed
by Antoni Gaudí, as were the heptagonal canopy above the high altar, the musical angels and
the choir stalls. Look out for the Portal del Mirador, the 14th century Gothic entrance.

39__ The Basket Specialist
The Mimbreria Vidal is a very special shop

Now this type of shop is not easy to find. Even in Mallorca this is probably the only one of its kind, here deep in Palma's Old Town. The Mimbreria Vidal sells anything to do with hemp, raffia, palm tree fronds or sisal. Off the beaten track, the shop has been run by its founding family for over 80 years.

Once, the Corderia had a whole slew of basketmakers, basketmaking being one of the oldest craft traditions on Mallorca, a skill handed down from generation to generation. Run by a father-and-son team, the Mimbreria Vidal is one of the last weavers of its kind on the island. Most of the merchandise is produced in the northeast of Mallorca, predominantly in the area around Artà. Here, women still master the art of weaving the palmitos, branches from the dwarf fan palm, and the Mimbreria Vidal still offers real handmade products for your money, making this shop indispensable for Mallorcans.

The shop is full to the rafters with hundreds of those woven bags that always make you feel like you should head immediately for the beach. In reality, these bags, made in various sizes and qualities, serve the Mallorcans in their general life, for going shopping at the market, as storage and, if there is nowhere else, even for a toddler to have a nap.

The Mimbreria Vidal sells practically everything: shopping bags and handbags, laundry baskets, fruit and wastepaper baskets, lampshades, rugs, hammocks and hats. The dominant colour scheme is beige and brown, but on request, bright touches can be added. Hundreds of baskets hang under the ceiling of the hopelessly crammed shop, as well as plenty of chairs.

One of the specialities of the family business is woven chair constructions, seats and back rests, which are still made here by father and son themselves.

Address Carrer Corderia 13, 07002 Palma de Mallorca. tel. 971/711243 | Access on foot, coming from Plaça Major or Santa Eulalia towards Plaça Coll, start of the Corderia | Opening times Mon–Fri 8am–1pm, 4–7.30pm, Sat 8am–1.30pm | Tip It is worth taking a look at the courtyard of the nearby 18th-century town palace of the Marqués de Vivot in Carrer de Can Savellà 4.

40___ The Bingo Hall

Flying balls of fortune at Teatro Balear

In Spain, bingo is a game for the masses. People love to step into a bingo hall even in the middle of the day. They'll take a break from their shopping, flee the heat of the city or spend their lunchtime here to take a snack and place a quick bet.

Bingo is popular, and entering a bingo hall is interesting for visitors to Palma too if only for the atmosphere, because here you'll meet all age groups and social classes. Of course, it's also fun to have a little gamble.

At the centre of the action are 90 light balls, each bearing a number, which are whirled about in an air passage then caught at the speed of lightning and rattled off one after the other – in Spanish of course.

Your job is to cross them off on the card you've bought, and if you don't understand the number, you can follow proceedings on the various monitors where they pop up. If you've got a complete row on your ticket, you call out »linea«; if all numbers are crossed out you've achieved »bingo« and receive the contents of the money pot. All monies are paid out right at the table.

One of the most beautiful bingo parlours in Palma is the one occupying the great hall of the venerable Teatro Balear, which was converted into a gaming hall 25 years ago. In the large theatre hall, Sala Balear, players sit in plush red armchairs around large marble tables. At the front of the hall, on an ostentatious gallery, sit the master of ceremonies, flanked by two mighty pedestals bearing the pyramids of bingo balls.

Electronic displays and numerous monitors keep the players up to date with what's happening. Tickets are sold by young women wearing short black skirts and tiger-print blouses, and once a new game starts you can hear a pin drop. If you like, you can just watch, take a drink and soak up this bizarre world.

Address Bingo Teatro Balear, Plaça del Comtat de Rosselló 4, 07002 Palma de Mallorca, tel. 971/711255 | Access From the Carrer Sant Miquel at the back of the Mercat de l'Olivar | Opening times Daily 10am–midnight | Tip Mallorca's one and only casino can be found in Palma's Porto Pi shopping centre at the harbour.

41__ The Bullfighting Ring
The Coliseo Balear is a listed building

For many animal lovers in Spain, and particularly in Catalunya, bullfighting is an anachronism and form of torture. However, for Corrida purists it represents a cultural highlight. Hardly any other mass event polarises to the extent of the fight – unequal in the end – between bull and matador. This holds true for Mallorca too. Amongst expats in particular, bullfighting is frowned upon, and there are plenty of tourists on Mallorca, forming the economic backbone of the Balearics. The Mallorcans don't enjoy having the permanent bullfighting discussion spoil this, bringing frequent public protests and demonstrations when bullfighting is scheduled at the Plaça de Toros. Because of this, the management like to put on other events in the arena, such as TV shows, tennis matches or open-air concerts, in order to take the heat out of any controversy surrounding the Coliseo Balear. The autonomous government of Catalunya has now passed a law banning bullfighting, but this is not the case for the autonomous region of the Balearics.

Bullfighting has a long tradition on Mallorca, and the Plaça de Toros belongs to the city like the Cathedral and the castle. Even when empty, it exudes an atmosphere of excitement and expectation. It doesn't take much imagination to see the snorting bull, the torero clad in gold with his red muleta and rapier, to hear the roaring crowd around the bloody spectacle. Maybe it'll bring to mind the bullfighting descriptions of Ernest Hemingway.

After some 15 years of planning, the Coliseo Balear arena in Palma was inaugurated with its first bullfight on 29 July 1929. Built by the Mallorcan architect and master builder Gaspar Bennazar Moner (1869 – 1933), the circular building harks back to earlier history. It is similar to an amphitheatre and inspired by the baroque style, measures some 45 metres across and holds over 11,000 people. To the left and right of the ring, at the entrances, tickets for shade and sun seats are for sale at different prices for »Sombre« and »Sol«.

Address Avinguda del Arquitecto Gaspar Bennazar 12, 07004 Palma de Mallorca, tel. 971/751634 | Access On foot, from Plaça d'Espanya through Carrer de la Reina Maria Cristina or Carrer d'Eusebio Estada or by Metro one stop to Jacint Verdaguer and then continue on foot | Opening times Thu from 3pm, visits are organised by Antonio jewellers opposite, tel. 971/295800, which also has further information. | Tip The new Palma Arena with velodrome at Passeig Uruguay 3 hosts numerous sports events.

42__ The Carrer Fàbrica

New gastro mile in Santa Catalina

On the other side of the canal, in the up-and-coming Santa Catalina neighbourhood, one street has developed into the trendy new in-place in Palma. No easy feat this, as competition is huge in this city so rich in restaurants, bars and cafés.

The Carrer Fàbrica, which got its name from the shoe factories that once existed around here, seems to have made it thanks to a few hundred yards of street that have been pedestrianised, planted with trees and declared a dedicated strolling zone. The locals are flocking here now, enjoying the nightlife far from the Old Town or the La Lonja neighbourhood.

Things start getting busy around midday, when tables are placed on either side of the pedestrianised area, but the real action starts in the evening and goes on well into the night. The numerous restaurants lining the streets include the Spanish Parilla Asador Txakoli with its Basque grill specialities, and the Italian La Bottega di Michele. The popular Fábrica 23 fish restaurant recently moved into the Carrer Cotoner, just a block further along and only a few yards from the Carrer Fábrica, a sure sign that the whole neighbourhood is evolving apace.

Santa Catalina is an old working-class district just outside the Old Town. This means a more modest architecture, smaller houses with a maximum of three storeys, younger yet no less charming than on the other side of the Passeig Mallorca. Perhaps it's this charm that attracts the young people, although the neighbourhood has an urbaneness all its own.

An important hub here is Santa Catalina's huge roofed market hall on Plaça Navegació with its impressive display of fruit, fish and meat and the numerous tapas bars and cafés along Carrer d'Anníbal. By the way, you can buy fresh fish from the stalls in the market hall and, for a small fee, have it fried for you at the bar.

Address Carrer de la Fàbrica, 07013 Palma de Mallorca | Access on foot coming from Passeig Mallorca above Plaça de la Feixina via Carrer Argentina; by public transport: bus no. 1 stop Argentina, bus no. 5 stop Passeig Mallorca | Tip At the corner of Carrer de Cotoner / de Bayarte you'll see an oversized, rather garish piece of graffiti covering part of a house wall with colourful representations of all kinds of international pop stars, and pointing to the rock bar »Exit« around the corner.

43 The Central Palma

An unusual youth hostel in the Old Town

The Central Palma is the most recent youth hostel to open in the city, privately run and different in many respects to the usual hostelries of its kind. The house has a modern, open design with a coordinated colour scheme. There are colourful objects and figures everywhere – whether tables, chairs or bar stools, everything is in colour. And the scheme continues in the rooms; for instance, the beds are all made up with linen in different colours.

Naturally, the youth hostel is intended primarily for backpackers and travellers on a budget, but all guests are welcome. Sure, it's not exactly luxury – the 20 doubles, four-bed and six-bed dorms have basic furnishings and usually double beds that all have access to the shared bathroom. Yet everything is spick-and-span and inviting, and many rooms have a balcony. This kind of corporate design continues in the dining room, the TV room and the music room with its piano. The courtyard too features colourful furniture, but also quiet corners where you can while away the time with the numerous board games. All the hostel rooms have free Wi-Fi.

The Central Palma enjoys a truly top location. The youth hostel is inside a former convent of the Franciscan order, which served as a school before conversion work started. Die Plaça Josep Maria Cuadrado is a picturesque square right behind the Sant Francesc church, not even ten minutes from the cathedral, and in the heart of the trendy Sa Gerreria neighbourhood with its large selection of bars and restaurants.

Central Palma's bar merits a special mention, with a good selection of reasonably-priced drinks to suit low-budget tourists, to be enjoyed on green and red bar stools inside or outside. Considering it's a hostel, prices aren't the cheapest on the market, but remain reasonable. 60 people can stay here, and most of the time the place is fully booked.

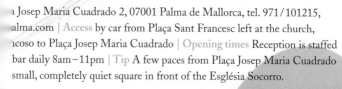

1 Josep Maria Cuadrado 2, 07001 Palma de Mallorca, tel. 971 / 101215,
alma.com | Access by car from Plaça Sant Francesc left at the church,
coso to Plaça Josep Maria Cuadrado | Opening times Reception is staffed
bar daily 8am–11pm | Tip A few paces from Plaça Josep Maria Cuadrado
small, completely quiet square in front of the Església Socorro.

44__ The Chocolatería

If it was good enough for Joan Miró …

Considered the best chocolatería in Palma, this café is certainly the oldest and longest-established place in town for a hot cup of cocoa. Since the early 18th century the same quality of chocolate has been served within its Art Nouveau décor, with a touch of the Biedermeier era, below colourful glass chandeliers illuminating swaying birdcages, filigree vases, copper kettles and wooden display cases. As suggested by the blue-and-white tiles in the café, the whole thing started in 1700 with Joan de S'Aigo's idea to bring down the ice from the so-called snow houses, or Cases de Neu, in the Tramuntana mountains to the town and sell it, enriched with chocolate, as ice-cream in the most fantastical creations.

Hidden in the narrow lanes of Palma's Old Town, the Choco-latería Ca'n Joan de S'Aigo near the church of Santa Eulalia is a high-light for any sweet-toothed gourmet. This oasis of chocolate usually serves the »black gold« as a thick liquid steaming hot in cups and drinking glasses – and in every variation you can think of. This is ac-companied by a miniature doughnut or home-made almond ice-cream. And better still, as the chocolate is so thick any spoon will stand up in it, you can dunk the always oven-fresh Mallorcan pastry creation called ensaïmadas into it too.

There is also a range of coffees, and cold drinks for refreshment, all at very fair prices. No wonder that come evening the chocolatería starts filling up with locals who will never let this café go out of fashion.

Artists have always been drawn to this place with its floor of green tiles adorned with palm fronds and the simple tables with their white marble slabs, and they would let themselves be inspired by the unusual, slightly kitsch ambience and the unique atmosphere. At times, painter and sculptor Joan Miró, no less, would take his hot chocolate here.

Address Carrer Can Sanc 10, 07001 Palma de Mallorca, tel. 971/710759 | Access between
Plaça Major and Santa Eulalia church | Opening times daily 8am–9pm, closed Tue | Tip
The Ca'n Joan de S'Aigo has opened a second branch in the newer part of town in Carrer
Baró Santa Maria de Grab. Diagonally opposite, Carrer Can Sanc 5 houses the avant garde
Teatre Sans.

45__The City Canal

A long history, yet loved by few

For years Palma's city canal, running down the Passeig Mallorca, was more reminiscent of a sewer than a civilised river bed. There was a bad smell and all kinds of rubbish was thrown over the balustrade – empty bottles, plastic bags, perhaps the occasional microwave or car tyre. All of which came into view clearly once the river bed had almost completely dried up, with only a few puddles resisting the baking sun. It was Palma's backyard, right inside the city. This has all changed now, and the canal has for some time been a true pleasure on the eyes, seamlessly fitting into the charming vista of the city that visitors get from the Es Baluard museum or the city wall.

Since the urban planners have ensured the supply of sufficient fresh water by constructing additional sluices, dams and pumps, the water once again flows through the stone bed, rushing over the cascades and playing around the pillars of the bridge. The deep-lying watercourse is framed by man-made banks planted with tall cypress trees and dwarf fan palms. The most prominent part of the canal, between the Avinguda de Portugal and the sea estuary along the Es Baluard fortification, works particularly well. The evil smells from stagnant water and rotting rubbish are long gone. And the citizens of Palma too seem to have made their peace with the once so unloved monster.

The city canal has been around since the beginning of the 17th century. With the construction of the large sea and city walls, the La Riera river diverted into the canal west of the city wall on the Passeig de Mallorca. Originally, today's Passeig de Born followed the course of the river, which used to wend its way through the town, and at the time of the Moors even served as the city moat. However, throughout the history of Palma this river was always more of a sewer canal than an aesthetically pleasing watercourse, and thus a public nuisance. Thankfully, today it is a different story.

Address Passeig Mallorca, 07012 Palma de Mallorca | Access Via the Passeig de Sagrera to the end of the city wall or from Plaça Rei Joan Carles I through the Avinguda de Jaume III to the Passeig Mallorca | Tip We recommend the nearby Dàrsena bar, where you can sit on the harbour in style, munching top tapas.

46__ The Courtyard of the Palace of Justice

A glimpse into the inner workings of the law

Officially, the courtyard of Palma's Palace of Justice is not really intended for the public, but it's still worth taking a peak. Although proper access is usually barred by a chain, you can still see a lot, and if you talk nicely to the guard he might let you step into the imposing courtyard for a few moments. Here, where today sits Mallorca's highest court of law, the Berga family resided from about 1670 onwards. In around 1710 they had the manor converted into a stately residence, and they claimed to have the largest patio in Palma. What is mightily impressive is the large set of freestanding steps through which you enter the building using entrances at each side, and which connects the individual floors of the palace, while the numerous arches bordering the courtyard are supported by Corinthian columns. In 1942 the palace was sold to the Ministry of Justice, renovated from the bottom up in the 1960s, and redesigned to suit its new purpose. However, the courtyard retained its typically Mallorcan character.

From the outside, the mighty building appears rather simple in style. What is striking are the two stone balconies, their massive footings and the conical balustrade. Above the doorway between the balconies you can spot the coat-of-arms of the Berga family.

The centre of Palma has some 40 patios that are worth seeing. Most of these courtyards were established in the 13th century, and originally they were appointed in rather simple Gothic style. It was only when the city started flourishing economically in the 17th and 18th centuries that the wealthy families had their courtyards lavishly redesigned in the Renaissance and Baroque styles, decorating them and adding water features. They were considered a calling card, a symbol of the wealth and social standing of their owners.

Address Can Berga Palau de Justicia, Plaça del Mercat 12, 07001 Palma de Mallorca, tel. 971/755369 | Access on foot at the end of Passeig des Born from Plaça Rei Joan Carles I via Carrer de la Unió or from Plaça Major via Plaça Weyler | Tip Do take a closer look at the old Grand Hotel, today the Fundación La Caixa, with its imposing art-nouveau facade, as well as the curved frontages of the two Edifici Casasayas houses, built in the modernist style between 1908 and 1911.

47___The English Bookshop
Rod only knows where anything is in this chaos

Not far from Plaça Santa Eulalia there is a shop that might be unique in all of Spain. »Fine Books« is the name Rod Browne has given to his English antiquarian bookshop, and the visitor is met by a flood of books and antiquarian bric-a-brac spread across three floors with nooks and crannies – if few windows – that you wouldn't expect in the Palma's Old Town.

It is not even ten years since Rod Browne decided to move his four antiquarian bookshops from Bournemouth in England to the Spanish sun island, partly for private reasons, partly because he'd long had a soft spot for Mallorca.

More than 1,200 crates of books were shipped over to Palma, where he found the right shop in the Old Town, »business space« for his unique collection of Old Things. Today, some 70,000 books, mainly English literature, military history, sailing texts and travel, maps including nautical charts, paintings, drawings, sculptures and all kinds of bits and bobs form part of the empire overseen by »treasure hunter« Rod. And new things are always added, from inheritances and attic clearances, or just books that tourists have finished with. But Rod doesn't just buy, he also sells, and he does so pretty successfully. »Reading is the cheapest form of entertainment« is his motto. If a client enters with a very specific request, Rod will dive into the apparent chaos for a few minutes, only to emerge again from the depths of the room with a dusty book and a big smile on his face.

Rod counts bibliophiles from all over Spain amongst his customers, as well as many tourists, of course mainly British. By now, the book shop is a tourist attraction in its own right. Rolling Stones guitarist Ron Wood, for instance, regularly drops by to browse Rod Browne's treasures. And he'll usually find something in the cabinet of curiosities of his passionate fellow countryman.

Address Carrer Morei 7, 07001 Palma, tel. 971/723797 | Access from Plaça de Cort via Plaça Santa Eulalia into Morei | Opening times Mon–Sat 10am–8pm, closed Sun | Tip A good »proper« Mallorcan bookshop is »Literanta« in Carrer Can Fortuny 40 near Santa Eulalia, with a bar and a cosy reading corner.

48__ The Espadrilles Shop

Handmade goods from the »Espardenyeria Llinàs«

This shop in the lively Sant Miquel street, lined predominantly with boutiques, galleries and elegant cafés, has been a family concern since 1927.

Which is when the grandmother of the current owner Marga Guilabert founded this little shop in a location that proved to be eminently strategic; Llinàs was the name of her mother. Espadrilles were always the bestseller in this rather understated shop, made by hand on the island and offered to the big-city buyers here. The red letters fixed above the shop read »Alpargateria Llinàs«, the Spanish name for the shoes. For the past few years the Catalan brand name has been added above, on a yellowish awning: »Espardenyeria Llinàs«.

The shop has two window displays and a rather inconspicuous entrance. All kinds of shoes are for sale, with the boxes reaching up to the ceiling, including a huge selection of children's shoes, plus, of course, every variation imaginable on the Espadrilles. Add to that handbags and the typically Spanish open raffia bags that tourists like to take to the beach. Inside the shop things are fairly chaotic, with open shoeboxes, shoes and bags hanging by the dozen below the ceiling of the two completely chock-a-block rooms, making it difficult for the customer to find a little corner to actually try on the shoes. There are sandals, comfy slippers, house shoes in leather or plush velour. Most of all though espadrilles, in every variation you can think of.

In fact the espadrilles are said to originate on Mallorca where they were the footwear of choice for fishermen and peasants. For a while they were all the rage in other countries too. The light linen shoe, usually worn barefoot, has long been complemented by new collections with leather uppers and heels, still sold under the Espadrilles name however.

Address Espardenyeria Llinàs, Sant Miquel 43, 07002 Palma de Mallorca, tel. 971/717696 | Access on foot from Plaça Major or Plaça d'Espanya | Opening times Mon–Fri 8am–1.30pm and 4–7.30pm, Sat 8am–1pm | Tip Across the street, a few paces will take you to the Mercat de l'Olivar with its permanent market hall housing a meat and fish market; a good option for snacking on a few oysters or tapas while exploring the city.

49__ The Flower Market

The Passeig de Rambla is Palma's flower mile

When the good people of Palma want to buy a substantial wedding bouquet, a weatherproof arrangement for the graves of their loved ones or just colourful flowers for the living room back home, they usually go to one of the dozen flowers stalls on the Rambla dels Ducs de Palma de Mallorca (»Boulevard of the Dukes of Palma«), which is now the full name of the Rambla. For the locals, it will always remain simply the »Rambla«.

Before you step onto the Rambla, via the large flight of stairs from the Plaça de Major and past two Roman emperors erected in 1937 in honour of fascist Italy and now looking a bit out of place, you pass an imposing concrete sculpture by Eduardo Chillida (1924–2002).

Created in 1975, »Lugar de Encuentro V« is one of a whole series of similar sculptures from the »Meeting Points« cycle. Since 1999 it has stood at the lower end of the Rambla, which, after about 300 metres in the other direction, is framed by a fountain.

The Rambla's huge, square, cream-and-blue paving stones, laid in a diamond pattern, are flanked on both sides by shady plane trees. Below, the permanent stalls of the flower sellers offer all kinds of kitsch vases, stuffed animals and ribbons alongside the flowers, which are mostly roses, bouquets, wreaths and funeral arrangements. The flower stalls are regularly interspersed by small cafés and newspaper stalls, while there are also benches for taking a rest.

To the right and left, the Rambla, laid out in the 18th century over a river bed that dried out back in the Middle Ages, is lined with busy traffic, but also by historic houses belonging to the wealthier citizens – the Iglesia de Santa Teresa de Jesús church to the right, and Santa Magdalena on the left. However, there are relatively few shops here, which is why this is not really a boulevard in the vein of a Passeig des Born.

Address Rambla dels Ducs de Palma de Mallorca, 07003 Palma | Access on foot via Plaça de Major | Opening times daily from 8am | Tip Between Plaça Major and Plaça Weyler, Palma's Teatre Principal awaits. A few yards on you'll reach the Forn des Teatre, Palma's oldest bakery with its art-nouveau entrance.

50__ The Franco Monument

Eternal argument around a dark chapter in history

Time and again the Palma municipality was reminded of the fact that there are still two dozen streets and squares bearing the names, on plaques and memorial tablets, of politicians and members of the military that formed part of Franco's dictatorship. But no longer – it's official. The clearest example of the new policy was provided by the city in 2010, with the Franco monument some 20 metres high, inaugurated in 1948 by General Franco and dominating the Plaça la Feixina. While the largest and most controversial monument of its kind on the Balearics was not torn down, as demanded by various victims' associations and pro-democracy initiatives, it was converted into an anti-war memorial. A compromise pushed through by those who saw a piece of Mallorcan cultural history in the monolith and insisted on keeping it at all costs.

All Francoist symbols on the monument were taken down and erased, and a rusty metal band was installed around the surrounding water basin. The letters die-cut into the band in several languages, including in English, read »This monument was built in the year 1948 in memory of the victims of the sinking of the cruiser Baleares during the Civil War 1936–1939. Today it is a symbol for the city of the democratic will to never forget the horrors of war and dictatorship. Palma 2010.«

Many Mallorcans reckon that this way of dealing with Franco's fascism is far from sufficient. Mallorca, which was conquered by Franco's rebels soon after the uprising against the Republican central government in summer 1936, always had an ambivalent stance towards the terror inflicted by the Franco regime. The Mallorcan bourgeoisie and the Catholic church were always on the side of the Francoists, muffling any opposition. It was actually on their initiative that the Franco monument was erected after the Second World War.

Address Plaça de la Feixina, 07012 Palma de Mallorca | Access Py public transport: buses no. 1, 21, stop Passeig de Mallorca or Carrer Argentina, on foot coming from Plaça Porta de Santa Catalina via Passeig de Mallorca beyond the city canal | Tip The monument for the victims of the civil war in Mallorca's cemetery is a fitting complement to this visit. The Plaça de la Feixina is a generously laid-out park, popular with skaters, featuring bubbling cascades, numerous artworks, palm and jacaranda trees.

51__ The Gargoyle on the Roof
Observing all citizens

Should you find yourself strolling along the dark, narrow Almudaina and hitting Carrer Morei, you might suddenly hear the sound of laughing from the distance. Feeling like you're being observed, images rise up and take hold, faces from medieval fantasies. Little wonder really, against this film-like backdrop. There it is again, this malicious sneering grin. No doubt about it, the sound is coming from above.

And when you look up between the tall houses and the gables you can make it out, dimly at least – the grimacing wooden face, the mask, the teeth, the beard, the pointy ears. Looking down on you from 30 metres up, below the wooden gable jutting out from this mighty city dwelling. Or is it all just in our imagination? Maybe the camera zoom might bring some clarity.

They say that these kinds of figures, mainly animal masks, were often affixed to gables or facades of houses to chase away bad spirits, but also sometimes to humour the spirits. And then you have the carvings, bursting with irony. One of the most striking examples can be found in Carrer Sant Feliu 10 in the lower part of the Old Town. This is where you pass the medieval house called Can Pavesi, which later passed into Italian hands and was given a new facade. Above the entrance are masks, gargoyles and a face half man, half lion. And that head is quite obviously poking its tongue out at you, in a gesture to those looking up and badmouthing or making fun of what they see. »For those who pass by« is what the signature says anyway. The house has since been called Les Carasses in Palma, which means something like »The Masks«. This kind of ornamentation on facades or buildings was introduced to Palma from Italy in the mid-18th century and initially used by Italian house owners as an artistic style element, before eventually being adopted by the Mallorcans too.

Address Corner Carrer Almudaina/Carrer Morei, 07001 Palma de Mallorca | Access
from Plaça de Cort via Plaça Santa Eulàlia into Morei and there on your left-hand side |
Tip In Carrer Morei, look out for the original English second-hand bookshop »Fine
Books«, a seemingly bottomless treasure trove, tel. 971/723797.

52 — The Grand Cappuccino
Stylish seating inside and out

Always well-appointed and stylish, the Grand Cappuccino coffee shops are a tremendously successful business idea made in Mallorca, which you might admire and respect without paying them too much attention.

However, the Grand Cappuccino in Carrer Sant Miquel, not far from Plaça Major, warrants a closer look.

Like many noble addresses in Palma, this café is housed in an 18th-century town palace, a building whose sheer patina of age gives it a special flair.

This Grand Cappuccino oozes with aristocratic class. Entering the café from the Carrer Sant Miquel side, through the large glass door below the row of planted balconies on the building's first floor, you'll immediately be struck by the genteel atmosphere.

The café is set up on the patio of a swanky town house, surrounded by an interior terrace, and spreads out below a rounded vault supported by columns. Via a freestanding set of steps you reach the first floor and its rooms furnished in different styles for special occasions, with changing art exhibitions.

Crossing the café and the building, you reach the heart of this Grand Cappuccino – a large garden with lush vegetation, its tables loosely placed around a fountain. The quality of the food and drink is excellent, the service welcoming.

The idea of the Cappuccino philosophy – there are a dozen of these cafés on the island now, all of them in top locations – was developed by British-Mallorcan entrepreneur Juan Picornell in the early 1990s.

Today in his early forties, he now has 400 people working for him. The Cappuccino empire in Palma includes the cafés Palau March, Borne and Passeig Marítimo. And the brand is happily expanding, including onto the Spanish mainland.

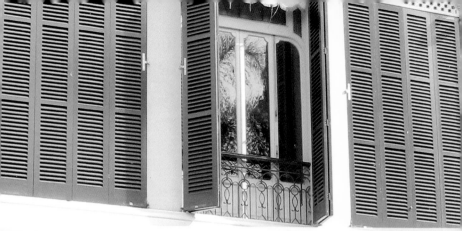

Address Carrer Sant Miquel 53, 07002 Palma de Mallorca, tel. 971/719764 | Access on foot from Plaça Major in the direction of Plaça d'Espanya | Opening times Mon–Sat 8.45am–10pm, closed Sun | Tip Before or after a drink at the Cappuccino, the Museu Fundació Juan March in the Sant Migue 11 town palace is worth a visit. The modern Spanish art on view includes works by Picasso, Dalí, Tàpies, Miró and Barceló.

53 The Grave of Ramon Llull

The father of the Catalan language rests at peace

On All Saints' Day 1490 spirits were running high in this slightly gloomy yet lavishly adorned church, the most important in Palma after the Cathedral. Out of the blue, records tell us, a dispute broke out amongst Palma's nobility, which escalated into bloody carnage. When Mass was over, some 300 dead bodies littered the rows of benches and outside the entrance to Sant Francesc. The reasons behind the feud have remained a mystery to this day. The whole thing was far from glorious for Palma's upper class, and maybe that's the reason Saint George, patron saint of Mallorcan nobility, is condemned to fight a dragon for all eternity with no hope of resolution right in the church where Mallorca's greatest son, philosopher and poet Ramon Llull (1232–1315) lies buried.

Not that it's particularly easy to find Llull's alabaster sarcophagus amongst the large, colourful stained-glass windows and the Gothic lateral chapels of this church. The burial site was designed in 1480 by Francesc Sagrera diagonally behind the altar and high up in a recess above seven arches meant to symbolise the seven arts and sciences of the Middle Ages. Lying recumbent and molded onto the coffin is the scholar and missionary. For his many philosophical and scientific writings Llull is also considered the father of the Catalan language.

In 1281 King Jaume II had allowed the Franciscan order to build the monastery and church in the centre of town. The crowning glory of the whole complex is the 14th-century Late Gothic cloisters with 115 filigree pillars and pointed arches surrounding the trapezoid courtyard with palm and cypress trees and a fountain. Today, this is where pupils from the Catholic school, run by the Franciscan order and considered one of the best in the city, often spend their breaks. The baroque facade of Sant Francesc, the imposing rose window and the portico with the group of sculptures created by Francisco Herrera, all date from the 17th century.

Address Plaça de Sant Francesc 7, 07001 Palma de Mallorca, tel. 971/712695 | Access
The entrance to the church is via the monastery seminary to the right of the church. |
Opening times Mon–Sat 9.30am–12.30pm and 3.30–6pm, Sun 9am–1pm | Tip The
monument in front of the church is dedicated to the monk Junípero Serra (1713–1784),
born in Petra in Mallorca, who left Palma to proselytise in California and founded the
town of San Francisco. The nearby church of Santa Eulalia is also well worth visiting.

54__The House on the Rock
Living on the edge

At the end of the 18th century, when Palma was still a far cry from today's cruise ship port, five close friends from the Old Town had the idea of buying a parcel of land outside the city gates to build a summer house. The idea was to be able to leave behind the hectic city at any time, in the evening or at weekends, to swim and relax. They dreamt of their own little summer residence and chose the plot above the rock at the spot where today you find the small marina of Gabriel Roca, opposite the Club de Mar and near the harbour road.

The new acquisition was parcelled up into five equal parts, before the friends figured out, over a few drinks, who was to get which bit. A fair and uncomplicated process, everybody was happy. So they had their five little houses built, and, as was agreed, had a continuous terrace laid in front of the houses, so they could visit each other any time, wandering from house to house, from apartment to apartment, in an open atmosphere.

After all, everything was owned by everybody. As the cut of the plot required, for practicality, the houses to be built in a single line, the last of them ended up so close to the rock that it was impossible to build a proper terrace there. The five quickly found a solution: to build a balcony on stilts in front of the house, with the terrace sticking out over the rock.

This provisional solution has lasted to this day, all strictly illegal of course, but quite romantic. Purpose-built steps in the rock allowed the friends to access the water and just jump in.

Today these houses are still inhabited by private owners. Although some of them have been extended over the years and converted into a hotel, this is also used exclusively for private rentals. The whole complex is called Portassa, which translates as the »big door«, just as the friends had wanted it.

Address Avinguda de Joan Miró 105, 07015 Palma de Mallorca | Access By public transport: bus no. 1, stop Porto Pi 8 (Club de Mar), Buses 102, 104, 106, 107, stops Gabriel Roca/ Porto Pi | Tip Why not visit the cruise ship harbour (accessible with bus 1)? A good view across the port can be had from the small courtyard and park of the Fundació Amazonia, Avinguda de Joan Miró 101, immediately next to the »House on the Rock«.

55 The Jazz Voyeur Club

Late night swing in the Old Town

Mallorca has a number of renowned jazz festivals, and big international names such as Chick Corea, Stanley Clarke, Ron Carter and Herbie Hancock have all made an appearance here. With the best festivals happening in summer, they are easily combined with a holiday. Sun and beach in the daytime, followed by sophisticated music in the evening. The Alcúdia Jazz Festival runs for an entire month, while other festivals are put on in the small mountain village of Banyalbufar and in Inca. Sa Taronja Jazz takes place in Can Burgos near Andratx, while the jazz sessions on Plaça Major in Sa Pobla are particularly popular with insiders.

However, since 2004 Mallorca's most popular and biggest jazz festival, drawing numerous international stars, has usually taken place in August across various locations in Palma. Jazz Voyeur is the name of the meeting, and it attracts plenty of VIPs. In 2006 the event organisers opened their own venue, the Jazz Voyeur Club, probably the most popular jazz club in town. Here, in the narrow alleyways of the La Lonja neighbourhood, things are full swing every night until the small hours.

Coming from Passeig des Born at the end of the entertainment strip of Apuntadores, with its wide range of tapas and cocktail bars, the bar is not much larger than your average sitting room. You sit in armchairs or on stools, mostly bathed in red light, or stand at the bar at the back. A beer is five euros, all spirits or cocktails a tenner. There is always a crowd pushing in, especially as often people have heard the sound from outside and quickly realised that it's well worth the entrance fee. But this doesn't lessen the atmosphere, and the Jazz Voyeur still remains a bit of an insider's tip, living mainly off its regular customers. While of course it helps to have some affinity with jazz, the concept has a relatively broad definition here – there might be blues, rock, occasionally funk or soul. Although jazz continues to dominate of course.

Address Carrer d'Apuntadors 5, 07012 Palma de Mallorca, tel. 971/720780, www.jazzvoyeur.com | **Access** from Plaça de la Reina into Carrer Apuntadores or from Passeig de Sagrera via Plaça Drassana | **Opening times** daily from 9pm until well past midnight, with often a second band coming on at 11pm | **Tip** Another hot spot for jazz aficionados is the Blue Jazz Club in the Hotel Saratoga at Passeig Mallorca 6. There is live music several times a week on the seventh floor of the hotel, with fabulous views across the night lights of the city.

56__The Knights Templar Signs

Emblems of a long-ago past

Initially called »The Poor Knights of Christ«, the order was founded in the wake of the First Crusade (1096–1099) and the conquest
of Jerusalem in 1118 near the Temple of Solomon. Originally planned
as guards for the protection of pilgrims and the Christian sites in
war-torn Palestine, the Knights Templar rose to become one of the
orders most shrouded in secrecy during the Middle Ages, were placed
under the tutelage of the Pope and became the fifth column of the
Vatican. Armed to the teeth, the force, at one point comprising over
15,000 men and seeing itself as a connection between religion and
knighthood, expanded towards Europe. And that included Spain of
course. Mallorca was one of the bastions of the order of the Knights
Templar.

In 1158, the Templars appeared on the scene, as the knightly order
of the Spanish Reconquista, the fight for the reconquest of the south
after 800 years of Moorish rule. The Templar monks with the red
crosses on their shoulder, reminiscent of the Passion of Christ, fought
loyally at the side of Jaume I of Aragón. After the capitulation of the
Emir in 1229 and Mallorca's transfer to Christian rule, the Templars
were rewarded with a quarter of all conquests. In Palma alone the Templars owned around 400 houses and 50 workshops. The hub of power
was the El Temple, probably erected in 1230 on a Muslim fortification
on Plaça de Temple in the Calatrava part of town, where some rem-
nants are still visible today. However, there is barely a guide that men-
tions the remains of the Templar Castle and the Templar church.

From 1308 onwards, the persecution of the Templars started all
over Europe. The Pope and secular rulers delivered the knights, who
had become ever mightier and more out of control, to the Inquisition
for charges of heresy and high treason. A few years later the order was
completely dismantled, and the Templar's possessions on Mallorca
were confiscated by Jaume II.

Address Carrer del Temple 9, 07001 Palma de Mallorca | Access from the Sant Francesc church through Carrer Ramón Llull into Carrer del Temple, or coming from the end of the Parc de la Mar through the Carrer de la Porta de Mar | Opening times The anteroom leading into the church, with information panels, is usually open for an hour from 12 o'clock onwards. In order to get to the church you have to ring the doorbell to the left and ask for admission. | Tip The altar image with Saint Bernhard o Clairvaux, one of the spiritual fathers of the Templars, which for a long time was housed in the Templar church, can today be found at the Museu de Mallorca.

57__ The Library in the City Hall

Discover a temple to reading in the Old Town

Whether for tourists or newcomers to Palma, this is a true insider tip amongst all the more conspicuous monuments the city has to offer. The library, with its wood-panelled ambience, is the perfect place for those who want to escape the touristic Old Town stress and find a refuge to read a book or newspaper, an international selection of which are available here. To get into the library at the end of the large city hall, you pass some figures of Mallorcan peasants, each a few metres high; their noble counterparts stand in another house further along in the residence of the island council.

Opened in 1935, the library was intended to serve as a beacon, signalling the shining path towards education open and accessible to any citizen. This, in any case, was the idea of the socialists and liberals in power during the time of the Spanish Republic. It was meant to open up education, often a preserve of the upper classes, to the large number of illiterate Spaniards at a time when libraries and bookshops were mushrooming all over the country. The library in Palma was kept open during fascism, but had to await the end of the Franco dictatorship to regain its full intellectual flowering. Here you can also find Palma's large municipal archive with a chronicle of the city's history and events, from the year 1206 to the present day.

Dating back to the mid-17th century, the impressive city hall features a projecting wooden roof, beautifully adorned. The three-storied facade symbolises the transition from Mannerism to Baroque, with, above the entrance gate, a large, impressive clock known as »En Figuera«, one of the first of its kind in Spain. The bench between the entrances to the city hall is a good vantage point for watching life on the Plaça de Cort.

Address Biblioteca Municipal de Cort, Plaça de Cort 1, 07001 Palma de Mallorca, tel. 971/225963, bibcort@a-palma.es | **Access** from the Passeig des Born on foot through the Carrer Constitició or from Plaça de la Reina through the Carrer Conquistador | **Opening times** Mon–Fri 8.30am–8.30pm, Sat 9am–1pm and 4–8pm | **Tip** Look out for the centuries-old olive tree on the city hall square, today closed off to traffic. To the right of the city hall, the Palau del Consell is a fairytale neo-Gothic building with turrets and garlands. This is the seat of the Mallorcan island council, the Consell de Mallorca.

58 _ The Pere Garau Market

A bustling slice of life far from the tourist trail

A visit to this market will show you a side of Palma that seems to have little to do with the big Mediterranean city. More like a North African scene, this is a slice of real life where, on market days at least, shopping becomes a social event. The Pere Garau square lies beyond Plaça d'Espanya, one more reason why very few outsiders find their way here. The offerings in this multicultural market place are excellent, both on the eye and the wallet. Punters come for the reasonable prices, but most of all for the quality of the merchandise. The housewives of Palma shop here, and the odd gastronomic star will also put in an appearance.

Palma's oldest market greets the visitor with permanent market stalls in a large hall. Long counters are laden with fresh meat and fish, and everything imaginable.

Here you'll have a hard time believing that parts of the Mediterranean are supposed to be overfished. The sausage and ham stalls will have you in raptures – Iberian delicacies, cut finely, packaged cleanly and handed over with a smile. Cheese stalls, pastries, knife sharpeners to ensure blades are always sharp for cutting the ham, stalls with little local delicacies to be sampled there and then, and a lottery booth to make your bets on the Big One, surrounded by so much culinary and visual fortune.

Twice a week, on Tuesdays and Thursdays, a big open-air farmers market is held on Pere Garau, where fruit, vegetables, plants and horticultural products dominate.

And then you have the twice-weekly animal market, which is a bit of an acquired taste, but very popular with many Mallorcans. On Tuesdays and Saturdays there is a cacophony of tweeting, screeching, crowing and bleating next to the large market hall, emanating from the tight cages containing hundreds of chickens, birds and rabbits.

Address Plaça Pere Garau, 07007 Palma de Mallorca, tel. 971/273283 | Access Coming from Plaça d'Espanya through Avinguda de Alejandro Rosselló, past the El Corte Inglés department store, into Carrer de Nuredduna, or through Carrer d'Aragó, turning into Carrer de Faust Morell. | Opening times Mon–Sat 7am–2pm for the halls, outside Tue, Thu 7am–2pm | Tip Further grocery markets in Palma are the Mercat de l'Olivar (Plaça de l'Olivar), fruit and veg: Santa Catalina (Plaça Navegació), fish: Llotja del Peix (Es Moll de Pescadores), Mon–Sat 7am–2pm.

59__ The Maritime Trade Exchange

Culture in Palma's finest space

This building is one of the most splendid that the old merchant's town of Palma has to offer. And yet many visitors walk past it, probably because for years it was closed to the public. This is no longer the case, at least when the former maritime trade exchange, restored from top to bottom over recent years, puts on changing exhibitions of contemporary art.

The large hall (in truth the single enclosed space), which in decades past also held legendary Carnival parties that insiders still reminisce about, gives the exhibits a flair all of its own with the light streaming in through the large windows.

Reminiscent of a cathedral in the Catalan Gothic style, the former goods and currency exchange, built from Santanyí stone with its six mighty lancet windows, eight turrets large and small, crenellations and patron saints for the ranks of individual merchants, was erected between 1426 and 1447 by Mallorcan star architect and master builder Guillem Sagrera, who was also much involved in the building of Palma's cathedral, as a hall for reunions of the merchants of Palma.

The city maintained active trade connections with a couple of dozen countries from the early 15th century until the 18th century. The ostentatious maritime exchange, a guardian angel watching over its entrance, symbolised the wealth and prosperity of Palma and Mallorca at the time.

In the 16th century, on a visit to Palma Emperor Charles V is said to have mistaken Sa Llotja for a cathedral. And it's true, the building extends across a rectangle 46 metres long and 28 metres wide, and inside six elegant columns across three naves fan out like spiralling palms, supporting the mighty vault.

Address Plaça Llotja 5, on Passeig de Sagrera, 07012 Palma de Mallorca, tel. 971/711705 |
Access from Passeig des Born via Carrer del Apuntadores and Carrer Sant Juan |
Opening times during exhibitions Tue–Sat 11am–2pm and 5–9pm (in winter to 8pm),
Sun 11am–1pm, at other times make sure you take a look inside through the large windows |
Tip The Plaça Llotja immediately in front of the maritime exchange forms a sublime back-
drop to eat in one of its many restaurants.

60__ The Museu dels Molins
On the trail of the island's symbol

There are over 1,000 windmills in Greater Palma. Most of those that you see by the dozen around the airport as you fly into the island would once have powered water pumps, essential for survival on an island with sparse vegetation. Then you also have a few dozen windmills that used to be flour mills. They are bigger and more solid and tend to stand on wind-exposed locations rather than on the plains. One of those locations is above the harbour in the El Jonquet part of town, a neighbourhood that started out as a fishing village right outside the city gates. These mills date back to the early 15th century, while most that you come across on the island, and that have become the symbol of Mallorca, were built in the 17th and 18th centuries.

The Mallorcan flour-producing windmills have a mighty square or rounded stone base, the so-called cintell, where the grain was stored, but where the miller would sometimes live too. The cintell is topped by the cylindrical tower rising some eight metres / 26 feet high and measuring 4.5 m across, with walls over one metre thick. A staircase would lead up through the interior of the mill into the roof, where the usually wooden sails were attached, connected by a shaft to the millstone below. Most windmill sails had six arms connected to each other with cross beams like a spider's web. Five of these windmills stand right by the sea along the harbour.

For a long time these mills had been falling into disrepair or were used as clubbing venues, and we have private initiative and the city of Palma to thank for the fact that these cultural monuments have in the recent past been restored to an acceptable state and become an emblem for the residential neighbourhood of El Jonquet, contributing to its increasing attractiveness. Inaugurated in 2005, the small museum in the d'en Garleta mill, named after the family who used to own it, presents the history of Mallorca's mills in an engaging way.

Address Carrer Molí d'en Garleta 14, 07013 Palma de Mallorca, tel. 971/280977 | Access
on foot from Avinguda d'Argentina, turning into Carrer de Sant Magí once level with Plaça
de la Feixina, then left into Carrer dels Molins de Migjorn | Opening times Mon–Fri
9.30am–12.30pm | Tip Four more historic mills may be viewed a few streets towards the
city centre, in Carrer de l'Indústria, at the corner with Carrer del Comte de Barcelona. Only
the first however still has its six-armed wind wheel.

61 The Musical Room

Where the March family made music

Once situated in the city, the March family estate stands now at probably the most exposed point of Palma, at the upper end of the broad stairway leading up to the Almudaina Palace and the Cathedral. The town palace, which since 2003 has been housing the Bartolomé March Foundation, son of the mighty tycoon Joan March, is entered via a huge courtyard opposite the battlements of the Almudaina. This loggia, surrounded by arcades and marble pillars, affords splendid views across the rooftops of Palma, in the company of numerous sculptures by Chillida, Rodin and Moore.

In the years between 1939 and 1945, Joan March (1880–1962), from a poor northeastern Mallorcan family who had accumulated a gigantic fortune through countless dubious business deals and political intrigues, built this town palace, which visually suggests more a 17th century palace. And when it came to designing the interior, the property speculator, arms dealer and banker really let rip.

In Josep Maria Sert (1876–1945), he commissioned the most famous Catalan muralist, asking him to paint the vault of the staircase and most of all the music room, which is probably unique amongst its kind. Large, undulating curtains hang from the walls, shimmering in silver and gold, incredibly airy and half-opened, but – and this is what provides the unique effect – made from plaster, cement and wood.

Tackling what was to be his last major commission, Sert adorned the walls and the vaulted ceiling of the music room with exotic musicians, acrobats, artists and masked dancers, full of a dynamism that took its inspiration from the jazz scenes of New York and New Orleans, as well as from the Venetian Commedia dell'Arte. Another highlight in the Palau March is the 18th century Neapolitan nativity scene, which is one of the largest in the world, featuring over 1000 figures.

Address Carrer del Palau Reial 18, 07001 Palma de Mallorca, tel. 971/711122 | Access from Plaça de la Reina via the Costa de la Seu staircase | Opening times April–Oct Mon–Fri 10am–6.30pm, Nov–March Mon–Fri 10am–5pm, Sat always 10am–2pm, closed Sun and public holidays | Tip The Grand Café Cappuccino on the lower ground floor of Palau March is very trendy indeed.

62— The Palma Artwork
Red letter city

The 3.7-metre-high sculpture between city wall and port, off the busy Avinguda de Gabriel Roca on Passeig de Sagrera, bears the name PALMA. Towering between the palm trees, tall as houses, lining the well-kept promenade along the city wall, the artwork features a pile of welded letters.

The PA at the bottom, the MA at the top, with an L set at an angle. The whole thing is made of iron painted bright red and embedded in a concrete base in a bed of roses. The sculpture has now become a kind of symbol for the city, evidenced not least by the fact that you can buy a souvenir version of the lettering made from solid metal in the Es Baluard museum shop.

Born in 1954, the Mallorcan artist Josep Llambías, whose numerous individual exhibitions, such as the »Septem« installation in 2010 at the Es Baluard, have caused something of a sensation on the island over the past few years, has become a firm fixture on the Mallorcan arts circuit. Installing his PALMA on commission from the city as part of the Summer Universiade 1999, Llambías masters a wide artistic range. Before discovering Pop Art for himself – which provides the artistic context for this sculpture too – he had studied landscape painting.

A few paces beyond PALMA you will encounter a sculpture created in 1953 by US artist George Sugarman (1912–1999), entitled »Negro & Blanco Horizontal«, another artwork installed for the occasion of the Universiade 1999. This is a curved black-and-white metal sculpture, inviting associations with a fish, or at least something from the sea.

All the artworks along the city wall give a taste of the Es Baluard museum of contemporary and modern art awaiting at the end of the Passeig Sagrera, whose range of high-calibre art installations make it an absolute must-see.

Address Passeig de Sagrera, 07012 Palma de Mallorca (level with Sa Llotja) | Access on foot along the Passeig de Sagera along the city wall | Tip In the immediate vicinity, the 17th-century Consolat de Mar building used to house the maritime court. In front, at an angle, you will find an all-white monument to writer Rubén Darío (1867–1916).

63___ The Rose Window

A morning glory of colours high above the sea

You simply have to see this window, these colours, this light. The sight of the great rose window of Palma Cathedral will stay etched in your memory, maybe forever, to be recalled whenever you want to conjure up the interplay of colour in Mediterranean light. In any case, this image gives an enduring veneer of refinement to any beach holiday or finca stay. With its 1200 coloured pieces of glass, fashioned into red, green, blue and yellow points and flowers, the rose window at the front of the cathedral, above the chancel, is unique and is considered a European highlight of Gothic stained-glass art, whatever your opinion on religion and the church. The best time to savour this spectacle is a sunny morning.

At over eleven metres in diameter, this 14th century masterpiece ranks amongst the world's largest roundels and forms the visual crowning glory of this three-naved church, which counts four more rose windows and more than 60 colourful pointed arch windows. The light-filled La Seu is also called »Cathedral of Light«. However, it wasn't always thus.

It was the Catalan art nouveau master builder Antoni Gaudí (1852–1926) who, from 1904 onwards, helped the church – left rather dark following various structural changes to the building over the centuries – rediscover the brightness and visual aspect that charms visitors today. Supported by the tall elegant pillars and the seemingly never-ending vastness of this sacred edifice, prettified by the light spots of the windows reflected on the walls, the mighty cathedral high above the city appears surprisingly airy inside. And this despite its dimensions: 120 metres long, 40 metres wide and 45 metres high. Over the centuries, the cathedral of Palma was the expression of Christian power, visible from afar on the open sea. In 1230 the Christian conqueror Jaume I of Aragón laid the foundation stone on the site of the hitherto Moorish mosque.

Address Catedral de la Seu, Plaça Almoina, 07001 Palma de Mallorca | Access from Plaça de la Reina via the large staircase past the Almudaina Palace | Opening times April, May, Oct Mon–Fri 10am–5.15pm, June–Sept Mon–Fri 10am–6.15pm, Nov–March 10am–3.15pm, all year round Sat 10am–2.15pm | Tip Take time to walk once round the building. The Trinity Chapel holds the sarcophagi of the Mallorcan kings James II and James III, and the museum with the church treasures, including two huge 18th-century silver candelabra, is worth seeing too.

64__ The Santa Creu Church

Palma's time-honoured house of God

While probably Palma's oldest church, Santa Creu (»The Holy Cross«) receives far less attention than the cathedral or the great churches in the upper part of the Old Town.

However, it is definitely worth a visit. What makes Santa Creu (or Spanish: Santa Cruz) special is that it consists of two churches really.

In the 13th century, the San Lorenzo chapel was built in the Early Gothic style on the foundations of a Moorish temple in the old seafarers' quarter high above the harbour. Today, this subterranean crypt with its freestanding columns lies beneath the chancel of the main church, as over the centuries Santa Creu was redesigned repeatedly.

With the congregation growing, the new, much larger church was erected above the chapel, and work on it would continue from the 15th century onwards. It was only in the 18th century that Santa Creu was finally completed, with a rebuilt main doorway and a splendid high altar, which is why the bell tower and the crypt of Saint Llorenc (San Lorenzo chapel) represent the oldest parts of the building today.

The crypt, which has its own street entrance, is only opened up for Sunday Mass. The ceiling of the main church consists of an imposing Gothic groin vault resting on octagonal pillars, while the walls are adorned with numerous Baroque and Gothic wooden panels. Santa Creu boasts an impressive Baroque organ built by master organ builder Damià Caimari in the mid-18th century, and also houses a museum with numerous sacred art exhibits from the island, including a silver processional cross from the Valldemossa charterhouse. The statue occupying pride of place above the entrance on the northern facade represents Saint Helena of Constantinople.

Address Iglesia Santa Creu, Carrer Sant Llorenc 1, 07012 Palma de Mallorca | Access The church is situated in the lower part of the Old Town on Plaça Porta de Santa Catalina in the immediate vicinity of the Es Baluard Museum. | Opening times Mon, Tue, Thu, Fri 11am – 12.30pm, Sun Mass in German in the crypt | Tip From the terrace of the nearby Es Baluard museum you can enjoy superb views across the harbour.

65__ The »See People«

Roger Löcherbach's wooden sculpture in
a reconstructed Spain

Exhibiting his work in 2008 could have brought great success to the German artist Roger Löcherbach. His unusual wooden sculptures, carved by chainsaw from huge tree trunks and mighty branches, were supposed to breathe some life into the village of Poble Espanyol, whose walls hide miniature versions, to scale, of famous Spanish monuments.

Visitors were somewhat surprised at who and what Löcherbach (born in 1963) and his curator had staged on the various squares of the artificial town, at the scantily clad group of tourists and the sun-bather on Plaça Major or the acrobats on the die Plaça de Santa Maria. However, Poble Espanyol never really took off, as the whole concept, thought up in the mid-1960s by architect Fernando Chueca Goitia (1911–2004) as an open-air »Spanish Disneyworld«, suffered some flaws from the start.

Across 25,000 square metres, visitors to Mallorca were treated to a medieval urban ensemble, which in more than 70 buildings, surrounded by a large city wall, was supposed to show what else Spain has to offer – from the Alhambra in Granada via El Greco's house in Toledo to the baroque tower of Torre de Santa Catarina in Valencia. An ambitious project in a city such as Palma, bursting with monuments and cultural prowess of its own.

In the end, when Poble Espanyol was restored in order to be reborn in 2009 as »Nuevo Poble Espanyol«, with shops and restaurants, hoping to be more attractive to visitors, artist Roger Löcherbach had to leave with his entire »troop« made especially for the show in Palma. Only one »Löcherbach« has remained: the wooden sculpture »Seh-Leute« – a maritime pun on »sehen«, German for to »see«, and »See«, the »sea« – of four wooden people, a little hidden away on the wall of Plaça de Santa Maria.

Address Poble Espanyol 55, 07014 Palma de Mallorca, tel. 971/737070,
www.nuevopuebloespanol.com | Access Public transport: bus no. 5 from Plaça d'Espanya
to Carrer Andrea Doria 22, then keep right | Opening times 9am–7pm, then restaurant |
Tip A footbridge takes you to the Congress Palace Palma, erected in the Neo-Roman style
with a »Sala Magna« reminiscent of a Roman basilica for 1,000 participants, as well as a
large Roman open-air amphitheatre for concerts and presentations.

66__ Señor Santiago Calatrava's Bull

Avant garde art on the city wall

The Bou bull up on the city wall at the Es Baluard Museo can be seen from afar and is increasingly becoming an icon of the city. The Spanish king Juan Carlos and his wife came especially to attend the inauguration of this unusual sculpture by architect Santiago Calatrava.

The day for the official unveiling of this gigantic bronze sculpture, consisting of 50 individual parts, on the roof of the Es Baluard was the three year anniversary of the museum, an important exhibition space for modern and contemporary art.

Weighing 30 tons in total and rising up to a height of 15 metres, the Calatrava sculpture consists of five cubes, each nearly 2 metres across and piled up skywards at an angle. They were delivered by several heavy trucks, lifted onto the wall using special cranes, mounted onto two stylised bull's horns and held in place by an ambitious steel construction.

The famous architect, construction engineer and sculptor is one of the stars of contemporary art and culture. Among his specialities are the construction of some spectacular bridges, of train stations and airport terminals, congress centres and theatres, as well as the opera house in Valencia, and high-rises such as the twisting Turning Torso in Malmö, Sweden. One thing common to all Calatrava constructions and sculptures is that they always move the viewer emotionally.

Born in 1951 near Valencia, Calatrava works with state-of-the-art technology, experimenting with ever new artistic forms. And it is almost impossible to amble past a Calatrava piece without feeling something. Many experts in the field consider the master of modern architecture the logical successor to Antoni Gaudí.

Address Plaça de la Porta de Santa Catalina 10, 07012 Palma de Mallorca, tel. 971/
908200, www.esbaluard.org | Access on foot, two minutes from Passeig Mallorca, buses
no. 1–7, 20, 50, stop Es Baluard and by Tourist Bus | Opening times The viewing
terrace of the museum, which holds the sculpture, is freely accessible. Museum: Tue–Sat
10am–8pm, Sun 10am–3pm, Mon closed | Tip The Es Baluard Museum of modern and
contemporary art is a must-see, showing works by artists including Pablo Picasso and Joan
Miró, Rebecca Horn and Gerhard Richter. It also has an unusual sculpture park.

67__The Solleric Café

Relax in style amongst cultural delights

Admittedly, the Bar Bosch – in reality a café that sits diagonally opposite on Plaça Rei Joan Carles I – is still the number one in town, and has been for decades. The main reason to be sitting here is to be seen – you are in the thick of things and the location is hard to beat. But the competition is hotting up, and in recent times, the Casal Solleric bar has turned into one of those welcoming cafés. Modern inside, yet with a cosy ambience, it also has a few outside tables right by the long established Solleric art gallery and now also right in the middle of the Passeig des Born.

This is a place which has managed to elude the masses so far, despite its flair, style, compact menu, gourmet snack cuisine, delicious daily specials and a solid choice of cocktails alongside all the classics. And of course this is an excellent place to start the day with a good breakfast. Since 2011 the café has been overseen by a chef much lauded on the island's gastronomic scene. And that is as it should be.

Casal Solleric, you see, is one of the top places for contemporary art in Palma, which means the café also works as a kind of museum eatery. After the city of Palma bought the baroque palace, built in 1775, from private Mallorcan hands and had it restored and renovated at no little cost, the three-storey building now houses Palma's arts centre, a bookshop and the central tourist information. With its elaborate windows, the marble pillars in the impressive patio and the free-standing staircase leading from the light-filled courtyard up to the first floor, the city palace at Passeig des Born displays modern art across several levels.

Alongside some permanent installations, international artists show their work in the large hall and visitors can catch changing art presentations on the first floor and in the enchanting medieval cellar. Some rooms still have the furniture of the previous owners.

Address Passeig des Born 27, 07012 Palma de Mallorca, tel. 971/722092 | Access on foot from Plaça de la Rei Joan Carles I, or, coming from the port, accessible from Plaça Reina | Opening times museum Tue–Sat 10am–2pm, 5–9pm, Sun and public holidays 10am–3.30pm | Tip On the other side of the Passeig des Born, the Garden of the Kings with its numerous fountains and sculptures is well worth visiting; look out for Joan Miró's bronze sculpture »Personatge« in front of the staircase leading up to the cathedral.

68_ The Son Moix Stadium of Real Mallorca

The home ground of Palma's most popular football club

Mallorca's collective football heart beats for the Real Club Deportivo Mallorca, RCD or Real Mallorca for short, from the capital Palma.

The club, which plays in the top league, the Primera División, was founded in 1916 and can look back on a long tradition now. The biggest successes were winning the Spanish cup in 2003 and making the final of the UEFA Cup Winners' Cup in 1999, where they lost 2–1 against Italian club Lazio. Playing in red and black, before the club moved into the San Moix stadium, which can hold over 23,000 spectators, Mallorca played its matches in the Luís Sitjar stadium, built in 1945.

The stadium was originally built for the XX Summer Universiade in 1999, which took place in Palma. This was partly an initiative on the part of the Balearics to change their image away from the exclusive focus on tourism. Once the Universiade had finished, the city of Palma handed over the stadium to Real Mallorca for the club's exclusive use.

However, the large multifunctional arena is also used for athletics meetings and pop or rock concerts. In late 2010, the Iberostar chain of hotels acquired naming rights. Since then, the stadium's official name is Iberostar Estadi, although most Mallorcans keep calling it Son Moix.

The second dominant sport alongside football on Mallorca is tennis, especially since the Manacor-born Rafael Nadal has become a living legend and is probably the most famous Mallorcan alive. Nadal achieved his first victory in an ATP competition in Mallorca in 2002. His victory over Ramon Delgado in the first round marked the beginning of a stellar career.

Address La Vileta neighbourhood, Camí dels Reis, 07011 Palma de Mallorca, tel. 971/221221 | **Access** Coming from Palma, the stadium lies right next to the Via Cintura motorway, exit Puigpunyent. The stadium is accessible by EMT public transport. | **Opening times** You might like to visit the stadium bar, which has plenty of Real Mallorca merchandise and can organise a tour of the arena. | **Tip** The Mallorca Tennis Club is a good contact when you fancy a game: Carrer Mestres D'Aixa, 07014 Palma de Mallorca, tel. 971/454717.

69___ The Sun Dial
A different way to tell the time

It is often claimed that Mallorca has the highest density of sundials in all of Europe. Experts talk of more than 700 timepieces of this kind, big and small, spread across the entire island right up into the mountain villages of the Tramuntana. You will find them at monasteries, churches, palaces and country estates, in parks and gardens, of varying sizes, vertical or horizontal to the sun, some painted onto chalk, others chiselled into stone. At the centre of operations is always the iron shadow stick, and if there's no sun, you won't be able to tell the time. If the hand of the sundial throws its shadow onto the number twelve, it's midday. While most sundials on Mallorca were made in the 17th and 18th centuries, there are many more recent specimens that are more decorative in character than aspiring to be serious chronometers.

In Palma alone there are about a dozen imposing public installations, some of which have been telling the time for decades, but only for those who can read them, as few people actually know how sundials really work.

Of course, it used to be different in the old days. For centuries, the sundials would determine the daily routine of the island dwellers, as people would read the time in this sophisticated but natural way, going by the position of the sun. One of the most impressive sundials in Palma, and one that many visitors walk past on a daily basis, is the specimen standing on the Avinguda Gabriel Roca below the Es Jonquet mills.

You will find more sundials in the immediate vicinity, for instance across the way at the harbour, where the colourful fishing nets are always spread out to dry, or at the start of the Feixina park. And last but not least, there is a huge great sundial cast from concrete, with a shadow stick as thick as an anchor, on the jetty of the old shipyard.

Address Avinguda de Gabriel Roca level with the mills of Es Jonquet, 07012 Palma de
Mallorca | Access in the extension of the Passeig de Sagrera, past the Es Baluard museum |
Tip Find Mallorca's most unusual sundial in the Santuari de Lluc monastery, the only
known multiple sundial, which shows the Central European, Babylonian and canonical
times simultaneously, on different clock faces.

70__ Sundown in Style

The finest views of Palma can be enjoyed
from Bellver Castle

No other spot gives a better view of the city and bay of Palma than the flat roof of the »Castle with the Fine View«, which ideally should be visited in late afternoon with the sun setting. Coming from Plaça Gomila, the route up through the Castle's own park of dense spruce and pine trees is already a pleasure.

There are benches at every resting place, with fantastic vistas opening up all around. And with every step you feel you are leaving the city behind, before it appears to you, breathtakingly, once you've arrived at the top.

From the outside, the Castell de Bellver, situated at 112 metres/ 367 feet above the El Terreno part of town, some three kilometres outside Palma city centre, appears like an unassailable fortification. It is flanked by three round towers half sunk into the wall and a fourth tower, offset a little and connected to the Castell by a pedestrian bridge. The circular courtyard is surrounded by a two-storey gallery with Romanesque arcades on the ground floor and an upper colonnade with Gothic-style lancet windows. As formidable and well-fortified as the castle, surrounded by a four-metre ditch, must have seemed to any attackers, the architecture inside is playful and graceful. That was exactly the idea when the Mallorcan king Jaume II had this castle built: to repel all enemies and pirates outside, while allowing for courtly rituals inside.

To this day, the Castell, built between 1300 and 1310 by master builder Pere Salvá, is considered one of Europe's most important medieval strongholds. Originally the summer residence of the royal family, Bellver served as a safe retreat in the case of enemy attack. However, just a few decades later Bellver became an infamous prison, the site of cruel persecution of Jews in the Middle Ages and, later, of bloody executions in the Spanish Civil War.

Address Carrer Camilo José Cela, 07014 Palma de Mallorca, tel. 971/730657 | Access Public transport: bus no. 50 (red city tour bus), buses no. 3, 20, 46 (via El Terreno), stop Plaça Gomila or Castell Bellver, by car: take the Carrer Camilo José Cela to the Castell Bellver car park | Opening times April–Sept. Mon–Fri 8am–8.15pm, Sat, Sun 10am–7pm; Oct–March Mon–Fri 8am–7.15pm, Sat, Sun 10am–5pm | Tip In summer, regular concerts are put on in the castle courtyard. The throne room and castle chapel are also worth a look.

71— Taking refreshments on the City Wall

Getting away from it all on the terrace of the
Es Baluard museum

While it's not obligatory to stop at the café on the city wall when visiting the Baluard Museum, it does kind of make sense. This unusual gastro spot high above the port will receive you well at any time of day, although best in the evening when the sun goes down over the far-away Bellver Castle, bathing the yachts and rooftops of the city, including the Cathedral, in a golden light. Taking coffee on the city walls, sipping a cocktail or enjoying a snack always creates its own special atmosphere, surrounded as you are by so many cultural delights.

The café was established at the same time as the Museu Es Baluard, serving as the museum café. While it has become a destination in its own right locally, it still remains a true insider tip. Some visitors like to sit under the large white sails, against the sun, or right by the wall or on one of the airy sofas and armchairs with their incomparable views of the palm-tree tops moved by the wind or Richard Hudson's bronze sculpture »Big Moma«, created in 2002. There's nearly always a little breeze, making this a particularly good spot to relax.

The name Baluard, meaning something like »bulwark« in Catalan, points to the original function of the building, which has been cleverly integrated into the old defensive works of Baluard de Sant Pere with Palma's Renaissance city wall. This move was all the more ingenious for the entire complex falling into increasing disrepair for decades. Today the old bastion in the city wall houses one of the most unusual museums in Spain, in a symbiosis of architectural styles from the 16th to the 21st centuries across 5,000 square metres. Modern art is displayed across several levels, from the crenellations of the wall to the former reservoir and port access of 1644, the Aljub – today a space housing spectacular art installations.

Address Plaça Porta de Santa Catalina 10, 07012 Palma de Mallorca, tel. 971/908200,
www.museu@esbaluard.org | Access on foot from Passeig Mallorca or from Passeig
de Sagrera | Opening times 1 Oct–15 June Tue–Sun 10am–8pm, 16 June–30 Sept
Tue–Sun 10am–midnight, bar/café tel. 971/908199 | Tip A little square worth visiting
for its cosy atmosphere is Plaça Drassana with its little bars and restaurants, coming from
Baluard at the end of Carrer Sant Pere.[S]PALMA

72__ The Tiled Wall

Joan Miró in XL

It's worth tackling the »descent« from the Cathedral down to the Parc de la Mar just for this. The huge wall ceramic by artist and sculptor Joan Miró (1893 – 1983) most definitely merits a close-up look. This is where the Tarragona-born Catalan Miró, who spent over 30 years of the second half of his life living and working in Mallorca, left his legacy shortly before his death in 1983. The tiled wall, twelve metres across and 3.5 metres high, is one of Miró's most important works in this form, ranking alongside the monumental tiled walls in Madrid, Paris and Barcelona.

The Parc de la Mar was laid out across several levels, below the restored city wall in front of the Almudaina Palace and the Le Seu cathedral, when the Passeig Marítim road running along the sea was extended in the early 1980s. The heart of the park, which features rows of palm trees, is a lake with a stage for putting on plays and other entertainment. The architects and artistic minds behind the park's design were Joan Miró and the urban planner Josep Lluis Sert (1902 – 1983), who also built Miró's workshop and studio in Cala Major.

The Parc del la Mar is a particularly fine spot from which to enjoy the extraordinary architecture of the cathedral and the Almudaina royal city palace opposite. The monuments seem to rise up sublimely in front of you. A good place for a coffee right next to Miró's tiled wall is now run under the name of Guinness House, with the bar inside in requisite Irish pub style. On the other side of the lake, changing art exhibitions are usually shown beneath the barrel vaults of the barracks built at the end of the 18th century, which border the city wall. Regular art events take place in the courtyard, many of them for free. The citizens of Palma like to meet under the colourful roof created by Ibizan architect Elías Torres, its harlequin pattern reminiscent of medieval street performers.

Address Parc de la Mar, 07001 Palma de Mallorca | Access by public transport: bus no. 15, stop Plaça de la Reina, a few metres from the Plaça de la Reina below the Cathedral | Opening times Park 24 hours; exhibition rooms May–Oct Tue–Sat 10am–1.45pm and 5–8.45pm; Nov–April Tue–Sat 10am–5.45pm | Tip If you feel like taking your drink by the water with a different perspective on the cathedral, head for the »Varadero« out at the end of the old port jetty.

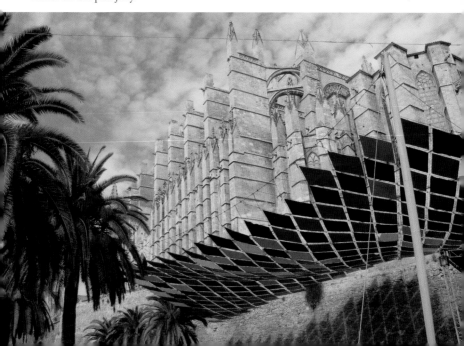

73__ The Train to Sóller

Take the island train through the Tramuntana range

Since 1912, the Ferrocarril de Sóller, also called »Red Lightning«, runs several times a day from the old railway station on Plaça d'Espanya in Palma to Sóller and back. Despite the name, it takes 60 minutes each way for the 27 kilometre / 17-mile tour through the Tramuntana mountains, one of the most beautiful routes on the island.

More than just a nostalgia trip, it's a journey back in time, as this is the way people travelled 100 years ago, and – leaving aside Palma, which has spread enormously – the landscape hasn't changed much over the decades either, as becomes clear when you trundle into the little medieval town of Sóller.

Of course, the trip is made nostalgic by the historic engine and the carriages with their mahogany wood cladding and brass handles. The original steam-powered locomotive was electrified in 1929. Built following an English model, the narrow-gauge railway goes through 13 tunnels, the longest measuring over two kilometres to traverse the Serra de Tramuntana, and passes numerous bridges and the Cinc Ponts viaduct.

Today, as it wends its way comfortably through the beautiful landscape, you can only wonder at the immense construction effort this train meant for Mallorca, with its scheduled stops in Son Sardina, Santa Maria, Caubert and Bunyola, before the mountains open up along the elongated hair-pin bends to reveal views of the Sóller valley.

The initiative for this railway came from the citizens of Sóller. In order to ease the ardous route through the mountains, and to transport and sell their agricultural produce, oranges in particular, more easily, they financed the train to the island capital and founded a limited company. To this day, many inhabitants of Sóller own shares in the train, which now finances itself through tourism.

Address Plaça d'Espanya 2, 07002 Palma de Mallorca, tel. 971/630130, www.trendesoller.com |
Access Nearly all city buses stop at Plaça d'Espanya. | Opening times The summer and winter
timetable may be consulted on the homepage, with the train running around six times a day. |
Tip From the Plaça d'Espanya (underground station Estació intermodal) another train runs an
almost hourly service between Palma and Inca, with additional connections to Sa Pobla and to
Manacor via Sineu.

74_ The Topsy-Turvy Chapel
There'll be no praying here

You won't believe your eyes at the Plaça Porta de Santa Catalina. Here is a small church on its head, the spire of the tower sunk artfully into the earth, as if about to topple over at any minute. This is a piece by US installation artist Dennis Oppenheim (1938–2011), who specialised in large-scale sculptures and expansive objects in metal, wood and stone. Oppenheim's sculptures can be found in big cities all over the world, including Palma, where the New York-based artist often spent time.

Standing on its head, the church made from steel, aluminium and wood, entitled »Device to Root Out Evil«, is a replica of an artwork that started its journey in 1997 at the Venice Biennale, versions of which can also be seen today in the Canadian cities of Vancouver and Calgary. Each one is different though, and constructed differently too, with the sculpture here, just under seven metres high, only the same as its fellow installations in other cities in general visual impact. This cheerily painted construction made from aluminium and wood is a prototype. Dennis Oppenheim is represented elsewhere in Mallorca with more spectacular artworks, including an over-sized painter's brush, one of the highlights of the Es Baluard museum.

The Oppenheim chapel has come into its own more since the Plaça Porta de Santa Catalina, which had degenerated into a grubby car park, has been converted into a graceful pedestrianised square, which offers up another interesting artwork: two huge granite pigeons who seem to have just landed amongst their fellow birds, pecking at crumbs. And when, in the evening, the small chapel standing on its head and giving out a faint blue shimmering light, marks one side of the square, and the mighty and illuminated Santa Creu the other, the square takes on the aura of something spanning different eras.

Address Plaça Porta de Santa Catalina, 07012 Palma de Mallorca | **Access** from Passeig des Born via Carrer de Sant Feliu and Can Sales or a few paces from the southern end of Passeig Mallorca | **Tip** We recommend the Es Baluard restaurant at Plaça Porta de Santa Catalina, serving upscale Mallorcan cuisine.

75__ The Turtle Fountain

Party with Palma's football fans

This is where the Mallorcans come to party well into the night, and sometimes until early morning, when Palma's football club Real Mallorca wins an important match in the Primera División or when the Spanish national team has been victorious.

On such occasions, thousands of people can be seen cruising around the Fountain of the Turtles, boisterously waving their flags and sounding their horns.

The Font de les Tortugues stands at the end of the Passeig des Born, the pulsating vein of the city, in the centre of Joan Carles I square and was erected in 1833 in honour of the Spanish queen Isabell II, just three years old at the time and starting her reign under the guardianship of her mother. After the queen was toppled in 1868 in the wake of political uprisings, the fountain was destroyed, only to be rebuilt again with few changes. Despite the thick, bustling traffic, it is most definitely worth taking a closer look at this fountain.

The obelisk, made from stone quarried in Santanyí, stands amid a large round basin and is crowned by a bronze bat, the heraldic animal of Palma and the Reconquista.

However, the truly special thing about this fountain is that the obelisk is supported by four turtles at each corner. The turtles and the small brass-studded lions' heads below them, are attacked on all four sides by permanent water jets shooting up around the rim of the basin.

Lined by dense tall plane trees, Passeig des Born forms the true heart of the city, with the squares of Reina and Rei Joan Carles marking each end. People meet on the »Rambla«, making use of the numerous broad stone benches, which towards evening attract mainly teenagers. At each end of Passeig des Born, two stone sphinxes watch over the happy throng.

Address Plaça Rei Joan Carles I, 07012 Palma de Mallorca | Access coming from Plaça de la Reina at the end of Passeig des Born | Tip Branching off the square to the left, you have Carrer Jaume III, Palma's most expensive shopping street, and the city's best gelateria, Ca'n Miquel.

76__The Workshop of Joan Miró

An atmosphere to inspire the budding artist in anyone

When Joan Miró transferred parts of his estate in Cala Major to the city of Palma in 1981, bringing it under the roof of a foundation, it was to ensure that his house and studio workshop, with his oeuvre permanently installed there, would not fall prey to speculation, as had happened in so many places on the island.

Born in 1893 in Barcelona, the painter, graphic artist and sculptor always had strong ties with Mallorca, until his death at the age of 90. The artist's family on his mother's side was from there, while his wife Pilar, whom he married in 1929, was from Sóller. Following long spells in Barcelona and Paris, Miró moved onto the island in 1956 to live and work. He commissioned his architect friend Josep Lluís Sert to build him the large-scale workshop, the Atelier Son Boter, which over the decades was to see the birth of era-defining artworks. You can still see it today in its workaday state, a treat for artists and the artistically-minded. And just as an aside, to the very left on the balustrade of the gallery hang the master's work clothes. The lower ground floor of Miró's residence, a finca he had converted, situated on a rise above the studio and surrounded by cypress trees, shelters more studio spaces, some of whose walls were painted by the artist himself and are decorated with objects of all kinds.

After Miró's death, his wife and the foundation commissioned architect Rafael Moneo to build a museum with sculpture garden and floating roof pool, which today is the seat of the foundation and with its constantly changing exhibits represents the core of the Miró-Fundació. All in all, the foundation owns over 2,500 exhibits by the artist, whose work comprises oil paintings, some highly colourful, sculptures, ceramics, collages and designs. Most people recognise his »España« design, which adorned the yellow, black and red logo of the 1982 football World Cup and today serves as the symbol of the Spanish tourism authority.

Address Fundació Pilar i Joan Miró a Mallorca, Carrer Saridakis 29, 07015 Palma de
Mallorca, tel. 971/701420, www.miro.palmademallorca.es | Access Buses 3, 46 from the
city centre | Opening times 16 May–15 Sept Tue–Sat 10am–7pm, Sun, public holidays
10am–3pm; 16 Sept–15 May Tue–Sat 10am–6pm, Sun, public holidays 10am–3pm,
closed Mon | Tip Near the Miró Foundation, at the beginning of Carrer Saridakis, the
Marivent Palace is the summer residence of the Spanish king. Although out of bounds for
visitors, you can still take a look at the entrance gate.

77 — The Place of Junípero Serra

The Mallorcan founder of San Francisco

If you were to declare that the big Californian cities of San Francisco, San Diego and Santa Clara had a direct connection to the small Mallorcan town of Petra, with barely 3,000 souls, you might be met with disbelief and incredulity. Yet it's true, and the signs are there in Petra, birthplace of the Franciscan monk Junípero Serra (1713–1784), who from 1749 onwards founded 21 mission stations in what is now Mexico, and from 1776 in southern California. These developed into important cities that have held on to their Spanish names to this day: Santa Barbara, Los Angeles, San José. But what is more, Serra is considered the founder of San Francisco in 1776, which also happens to be the year of the United States' Declaration of Independence. And this is why the US Capitol building in Washington holds his bust amongst great American heroes. Today, Petra is particularly proud of this, and of the fact that Junípero Serra, who died and was buried in California in 1784, was beatified in 1988 by Pope John Paul II. And just in passing, Junípero Serra, son of a simple peasant, is also said to have brought viniculture to California, in the mission station of San Diego. In Petra too, winemaking is the basis of many people's livelihood.

Not far from the tiny whitewashed birthplace of this small town's greatest son, in Barracar Alt, the oldest part of the town, a museum built in 1959 documents the monk's missionary work. In the 17th century church of Sant Pere you can still see the Gothic baptismal font over which the young Serra would have been held, and the wall is adorned with a large memorial plaque. The boy would have been educated in the Convent de Sant Bernardí monastery school. The Plaça del Padre Serra has a monument to him, and in Carrer Fra Junípera you'll encounter colourful tiled images depicting the eventful life story of the monk from Petra, who joined the Franciscan order aged only 16.

Address Casa Natal i Museu Junipero Serra, Carrer Barracar Alt 6–8, 07520 Petra, tel. 971/561149 | Access by car: Petra lies on the main Ma-3320 road from Manacor in the direction of Inca. | Opening times Opening times are irregular. If the museum is closed, a panel lets visitors know where to pick up the key. | Tip Next to the church of San Pere, a large monument honours the women farmers of Mallorca. A few miles outside Petra, on a hill, discover the Ermita de Bonany hermitage with its legendary Madonna.

78__The Hipica Formentor Stables

An alternative ride through unspoilt landscapes

There are plenty of stables on Mallorca. You can take classes, individual lessons or book a package, with or without accommodation, hire a horse for the hour or the day, have treks organised for you, or simply take a break from the beach holiday for a few hours. There is everything, from the traditional riding school to pony farm. So far so conventional, if it wasn't for the Hipica Formentor Stables, which tries to do everything differently from the competition. Although they do ride here of course, and how.

On the edge of the S'Albufereta nature reserve near the Bay of Pollença, the stable's 25 horses are allowed to roam free in a herd, unshod and, more unusual still, ridden without a bit, rather with a snaffle that is not placed in the horse's mouth. This fits with the life philosophy of Mallorcan Lorenzo, who grew up with horses and was stationed for years in Newmarket, the equine centre in the east of England, and his wife Christiane. For over 15 years now they have practised the natural way to keep horses. And on their little farm they have quite a colourful equine mix. This is because one of Lorenzo's specialities is to rescue discarded or sick horses on the island, take them in and gradually teach them to trust people again, in order to ride them. »Natural Horsemanship« is what he calls this. It takes a lot of gentleness and skill, and there are people who credit Lorenzo with the quality of the proverbial »horse whisperer«. Of course, riding still remains important.

Hipica Formentor's speciality is treks into the mountains, for instance, along the pilgrim trail to Lluc or onto the Puig Galileo through dried-out river beds, from overnighting in the monastery to rides lasting a few hours or an entire day bordering the Albufereta nature park.

Address Finca Can Bobis, 07470 Pollença, mobile tel. 609/826703,
www.hipicaformentor.com | Access Travelling on the Ma-2200, take the exit marked
Bahia de Pollença at the roundabout with the »large cockerel« just before reaching
Pollença, and look out for signs for »HF Horseriding«, or from the Ma-2220 Port
d'Pollença–Alcúdia, exit just past the Can Curasa restaurant, follow the signs. |
Opening times all day, best to phone ahead | Tip At the nearby Bay of Alcúdia, the
Ranxo ses Roques horse farm (tel. 971/892809, www.ranxosesroques.com) offers
another opportunity for treks by the hour.

79__The Pilgrimage Trail
A meditative trip to the Black Madonna

»Lluc on foot« is a common expression in Mallorca, meaning that there is hardly a family on the island who haven't sent at least one of their members on a pilgrimage to the Lluc monastery. High up in the Tramuntana range, the monastery is in fact the spiritual centre of the island. A pilgrimage to Lluc in honour of the Black Madonna really is a rite of passage for any Mallorcan serious about their religion. In summer, hundreds of them roam thorough the Tramuntana mountains, happily singing and making penance, in order to worship at the feet of the Mare de Déu de Lluc and rest afterwards at the monastery's restaurant or take a picnic at one of the large barbecue sites. Many pilgrims choose to stay overnight in one of the simple rooms on offer at the monastery guesthouse.

Especially charming, and not too onerous, is the historical pilgrimage route. At nearly 14 kilometres long, from Pollença to Lluc, the trail starts near the old Roman bridge, the Pont Romà. It takes about four-and-a-half hours to walk this classic pilgrimage route to the monastery, situated some 500 metres above sea level, and it's an easy walk, more like an rarefied stroll through a magnificent landscape. You pass the Puig Tomir and orange groves, cross over passes and brooks, and walk through holm oak forests.

People have been making the pilgrimage to the Black Madonna with baby Jesus on her left arm, or, as she is called by the Mallorcans, the Little Black One, since the Reconquista. In 1229 the shepherd boy Lluc is said to have found the statue on the spot where the monastery stands today, and taken it to the priest of the church at Escora. But the Madonna disappeared overnight, returning to its original spot. Once this mysterious performance had repeated itself a few times, it was taken as a hint from above and a small chapel was eventually built at the spot where the Black Madonna was found, the foundation stone for Lluc Monastery.

Address Long-distance trail 221 at Pont Romà, 07460 Pollença | **Access** take the Ma-13 past Sa Pobla and then the Ma-2200 to Pollença | **Opening times** Lluc Monastery is open all day. | **Tip** Before you start walking, take a look at the old Roman bridge, Pont Romà. Inside Lluc Monastery, it is worth taking in the museum, displaying numerous exhibits on archaeological finds and the history of Lluc.

80__ The Steps

A step for every day of the year

There is something extraordinarily sublime about taking the 365 natural-stone steps up the Calvary hill, enough to take the most romantic soul by surprise. Three hundred and sixty-five steps – one for every day of the year – lined by cypress trees, pine trees and cacti. And at the top the baroque El Calvari church, built in 1795, with its wide terrace.

Up here, the view of Pollença is captivating – the ochre-coloured rooftops, the Puig de Santa Maria opposite, the expansive orchards along the usually dried-up Torrent de Sant Jordi river, and onto the plain all the way to the sea, with the bays of Pollença and Alcúdia.

Leaving the hilltop once more to saunter down the same long set of steps in the direction of Plaça Major, another exquisite view of the town and mountains opens up. And with it the prospect, once back in the city centre, of a visit to one of the cafés on Plaça Major.

On Catholic feast days, processions lead up the Calvary hill. On Maundy Thursday for instance, the Cross of Christ is carried up those 365 steps along the stations of the cross onto the 170m / 558-ft Puig de Calvari, to be taken down again symbolically in the late evening of Good Friday, accompanied by drums, to the parish church of Nostra Senyora dels Angels.

The Puig de Calvari has been revered since the mid-13th century, when, according to the choniclers, shipwrecked castaways from Cala Sant Vincenç erected a cross high up here above the settlement out of gratitude for their salvation.

The Calvary hill, which, following the Reconquista and the foundation of the town of Pollença in the early 13th century, passed into the possession of the Order of the Knights Templar, who established it as a religious site, is one of the most important of its kind in all of Spain.

Address Puig de Calvari, 07460 Pollença | Access Take the Ma-13 past Sa Pobla, then the Ma-2200 to Pollença | Opening times Always accessible | Tip The Museu Martì Vicenç at the foot of the Calvary hill, with works by the artist of the same name, is worth a visit. On Sundays, a colourful fruit and veg market takes place on Plaça Major.

81__ The Canal of Albufera
Unspoilt nature away from the tourist resorts

What seems like pristine nature today, like an oasis of primeval scenery amidst an increasingly urbanised landscape, a coastal strip slowly disappearing under the concrete of encroaching resorts, has actually already been subject to substantial human intervention. The Parc Natural S'Albufera, covering 1,700 hectares, making it the Balearics' largest area of swamp and an official nature reserve since 1988, was originally a large inland freshwater lake cut off from the sea by dunes, which slowly silted up over the millenia, but without ever drying out completely.

Albufera, from the Arabic word for lagoon, »Albuhayra«, became a huge swamp area whose margins have been used for agriculture since the time of the Romans, and whose people always had to fight the lethal malaria caused by mosquitoes. As early as the 17th century, the local population tried to tame the swamp by digging small canals.

However, the really ambitious attempt was made in the mid-19th century by the British Majorca Land Company with its engineer Frederick Bateman. Planning to use the entire area for industry and agriculture, he employed well over 1,000 workers to dig an extensive network of canals, 400 km / nearly 250 miles long, which would receive the fast-flowing waters of the Torrent de Muro and de Sant Miquel. In the end, Bateman and his company failed, because the constant seeping-in of seawater made the drying out of the area – situated below sea level – an impossible task. The largest of these artificial drainage canals at 60 metres / 65 yards wide, the Canal Gran de s'Albufera runs for 2.5 km / 1.5 miles through today's nature reserve – eventually emptying into the sea beyond the Pont dels Anglesos or »Bridge of the English« – along the road from Port Alcúdia to Can Picafort near s'Oberta, cutting a broad swath through the landscape.

Address Carretera Alcúdia–Artà, 07458 Platjes de Muro | Access Take the Ma-12 from
Port d'Alcúdia to Ca'n Picafort, park on the bridge just before you get to the Hotel Parc
Natural, then walk about a kilometre / under a mile, keeping right, to the visitor centre;
buses 353, 354, 355 from Pollença and Alcúdia, stop Parc Natural | Opening times Parc
Natural S'Albufera April–Sept 9am–6pm, Oct–March 9am–5pm, Sa Roca visitor centre
daily 9am–4pm | Tip Shortly before you get to the bridge, head along the canal to the
Sa Roca visitor centre, the gateway to the S'Albufera nature park; the most beautiful time
for visiting is the early morning. There is another, smaller nature reserve between Alcúdia
and Pollença, the S'Albuferata de Pollença swamp.

82__ The Power Station

An industrial monument looking for a new use

The contrast could hardly be more pronounced. The picturesque landscape, with ruins from Roman and Moorish times, old monasteries and enchanted churches, historic city walls, the marina with its elegant pleasure boats, hidden bays and inviting sandy beaches – all pure nature, and smack-bang in the middle of it a hulking piece of a more recent industrial landscape. Shut down a few years ago, for decades the coal plant of Alcúdia was considered a symbol of progress on the island, which had always lived mainly from agriculture until the advent of tourism brought a dramatic upturn in economic fortunes.

Today, historical heritage old and new is looked after. Consequently, the old coal plant has now been declared an industrial monument, only no one is quite sure what to do with it. One thing is certain though: it won't be pulled down, as many have demanded, and its future lies in cultural use. In any case, the plant is already a sight in its own right, warranting a stop and good look around. However, for the time being it remains an industrial ruin, visible from afar, fenced-off and strictly guarded, with the two huge chimneys making a pithy statement.

Historically, Alcúdias' economic situation has been quite chequered, experiencing a short boom with the expansion of the port for international trade in the late 18th century. However, the true upturn for the region, and with it the whole of Mallorca, was triggered in large part by the coal plant built in 1957 in the port of Alcúdia, just before the turn off to Alcanada, which was to provide the entire island with electricity. The plant remained operational into the 1980s, before eventually being replaced, as tourism became the island's main source of income, by a plant erected far beyond the bay. Equally visible from afar, along the road to Sa Pobla, today this provides electricity for the island.

Address Carrer del Moll Comercìal, 07400 Port d'Alcúdia | **Access** By car, from Port d'Alcúdia on the Ma-2200 immediately before the turn-off to Alcanada | **Tip** The new coal plant can easily be seen along the Ma-3433.

83___The Barbara Weil Studio

A studio built by famous architect Daniel Libeskind

Who knows whether US artist Barbara Weil would have gained as much attention had she not thought to harness internationally renowned star architect Daniel Libeskind for the construction of her studio. Born in Chicago in 1933 and living and working on Mallorca since the early 1970s, the artist can actually look back on an impressive oeuvre, which she is still expanding tirelessly, having stayed remarkably active and creative. Working in painting, sculpture and modelling, her multidimensional fibreglass sculptures, sometimes strident and colourful, are acknowledged far beyond the island and achieve high prices.

However, the name only really came to the attention of a broader public and the wider art world once she developed, together with Daniel Libeskind, the idea of having a studio built with gallery onto her former tennis court next to the house where she lived. The result was this ambitious structure which has become a fixture in Port d'Andratx, providing a glorious counterpoint to all the identikit urban developments and illegally built houses on the hill slopes surrounding the picturesque harbour.

Erected in 2003 along the road to the La Mola residential neighbourhood of villas, the Studio Weil is a highly successful symbiosis between art and architecture. The creator of the extravagant Jewish Museum in Berlin and main architect of the redesign of Ground Zero in New York has created an unorthodox structure full of interior angles, with plenty of space for art. It gives the artist's sculptures and paintings room to breathe and is forever providing new perspectives to the visitor: curves, slants, trademark Libeskind windows and surprising light effects. The Studio Weil, this total work of art, or »gesamtkunstwerk« of outer shell and content, features a large jagged window, in which the artist's works welcome the visitor.

Address Camí de Sant Carles 20, 07157 Port d'Andratx, tel. 971/671647, www.studioweil.com | **Access** Take the Ma-1 from Palma to Port d'Andratx | **Opening times** Sat, Sun 11.30am−2pm, 4−6pm (by appointment) | **Tip** The nearby little town of Andratx with its 13th-century parish church of Santa Maria is well worth visiting, as is the Centro Cultural Andratx, a privately run cultural institution with studios, gallery and changing exhibitions.

84_ The Museum of the Sea
Centuries of fighting pirates

High up on a rock formation on the outermost edge of the Bay of Port d'Sóller, at the northern end of the historical fishing quarter of Santa Catalina, you will encounter a former 13th century chapel, the El Oratori de Santa Caterina d'Alexandria. Once a shelter for those who became stranded here, and connected with the adjacent monastery, the entire complex was turned over to the military and was off limits to the public for decades.

Today it holds the Museu de la Mar, the only one of its kind on the island.

The museum tells the story of Port de Sóllers, this near-circular natural port protected on both sides by rock formations, which lent it a certain sense of protection over the centuries and where the people would usually feel secure on an island with an eventful history. The Miranda de Santa Caterina watchtower always provided sweeping views across the seas in order to identify incoming ships early, and to set up the cannons if they brought plundering pirates, as was often the case.

The museum documents this fight against piracy, with the cannons from that time still standing, and there is also plenty about fishing, especially the whaling that went on for centuries here. You might get the chance to witness the fishermen in the back part of the harbour with the catch of the day around 5pm, with the restaurant owners fighting over the best goods and the colourful fishing nets spread out to dry – the museum tells exactly this story, of the eternal life with the sea.

And it documents the harbour's heyday, when there was no rail connection and crossing the Tramuntana range was arduous and time-consuming in the extreme, when the steamboats laden with oranges would set sail to take the »gold« of the fertile valleys around Sóller to France or to the capital Palma.

Address Carrer Santa Catalina d'Alexandria 50, 07108 Port de Sóller, tel. 971/632204 | Access By car: drive to the harbour and continue on foot from the jetty to the viewing platform | Opening times Tue–Sat 10am–6pm, Sun, public holidays 10am–2pm, closed Mon | Tip From the harbour, boats leave for the Cala de Sa Calobra and the captivating estuary of the fast-flowing Torrent de Pareis.

85 __ The Tower

Watching over all those yachts

Now almost one geographical entity, the resorts of Portals Nous and Bendinat, southwest of Palma, are arguably the fanciest on the island. This is where those with plenty of money like to congregate. Some hide behind their ample estate walls and dense bougainvillea hedges, while the more nouveau-riche like to put their wealth on show along the yacht and harbour strip. Anyone who's anyone, or believes themselves to be, moors their luxury boat here in Port Portals, with some even having a fixed mooring. The marina of Portals Nous, you see, is the most exclusive on the whole of Mallorca, and must rank amongst the top five in Europe with regards to the size and appointment of boat, and with this of course the price. And in order to underline this fact, many of the yachts have matching fine limousines parked outside, often with chauffeur, signalling that the owner is on board. If they are not shopping in the exclusive arcades or taking lunch in the restaurant Tristán Mar. And if the owners are not around, the crew will be scrubbing and cleaning the planks and the deck. Depending on the size of the boat, moorings cost between 500 and 1,000 euros per night. Free spaces are rare though, as the waiting list is always long.

For the ordinary tourist to Mallorca a detour to Portals Nous is worth it if only for the extraordinary boats. And a drink on the promenade is affordable too. In any case, Portals Nous represents a major contrast to the all-inclusive kind of tourism.

And who watches over all this luxury and some 700 yachts up to 60 metres long, costing an average of two-and-a-half million euros, some of them ten or more (take a look at the notices in the boat agency windows). The harbour tower does. But none of this is very old – the Marina Portals, the jetties, mooring spaces, buildings and the harbour tower itself, whose entrance is still crowned by the ship's bell that inaugurated operations, were only laid out in 1986.

Address 07181 Portals Nous | Access Ma-1 Palma−Andratx, exit Portals Nous | Tip The terrace with the excellent restaurant of the nearby Hotel Bendinat is worth a visit. A trendy choice is the Grand Café Cappuccino on the left, at the **access** road to the port. The Castell de Bendinat may be viewed too, if only from the outside.

86__ The Stone Quarry

*Sun and swimming at one of the island's
most unusual spots*

A few years ago, all this was much more remote and unspoilt. At the time, the rugged coastline deep below the plateau of Puig de Ros was harder to reach and not really considered a holiday destination. This changed once the area between the Ma-6014 coastal road, from S'Arenal to Cala Pi, and the sea was allocated as land for construction and built on accordingly.

Today, large settlements have encroached on the coastal side, some with rather identikit houses and all with pool, intended less for tourists than for Mallorcans. Although there are no proper beaches here in the classic sense, but more a steep, craggy coast, this is in fact what attracts many people.

So it might come as no surprise to hear that insiders swear by this rocky strip of coast as one of the island's most attractive areas for swimming and soaking up some sun.

And there is a good reason for this. These bizarre rock formations did not come about entirely naturally over millions of years, but with man's helping hand. For decades stones were broken, smashed and sawn here, probably including those used in the building of Palma cathedral. These were truly enormous rectangular blocks, transported to the capital on barges (at the time, the cathedral still bordered the sea directly). For generations, thousands of people worked at completing this monumental Gothic construction, and the steep coast south of what is today S'Arenals was chosen as the nearest quarry.

Today then, as you take the narrow footpaths left and right through the shrubs, below the car park and the offshore Mhares Sea Club, you can lie down at your leisure on the flat rock formations and blocks of Marès stone, in the knowledge that they were cut and shaped by human hand.

Address Carrer del Oronella, 07609 Puig de Ros (Llucmajor) | Access Coming in on the Ma-4016 from S'Arenal level with the Maiorís golf course (at km 6), turn off left to Puig de Ros and continue on to Mhares Sea Club | Opening times Accessible anytime, public car park | Tip The Mhares Sea Club, part of the nearby Delta Hotel, is accessible to anyone for a day-fee and enjoys a quite privileged location.

87__The Swallow's Nest

Monastic treasures on the holy mountain

Only in Randa will you find a hill that looks like a table mountain, boasting three monasteries at different altitudes. All of which makes this 542m/1778-ft elevation, visible from afar when crossing the Mallorcan plain of Es Plà, the rightful holy mountain and Mallorca's most important pilgrimage site after Lluc. The first thing you see, approaching the mountain on a hairpin bend road leading up from the village of Randa, is the »Swallow's Nest«, a little whitewashed monastery stuck onto the mountainside. The small chapel behind the cross at the entrance and the sanctuary of Santuari de Nostra Senyora de la Gràcia were built onto the mountain in the 15th century below a towering rockface. A visit to the small church is worth it for the Virgen de Gràcia, an image of the Virgin Mary by Mallorcan sculptor Gabriel Mòger, who is much revered on the island. Following a landslide in 2005 and the temporary closure of the »Swallow's Nest«, the monastery has been restored and renovated.

About one kilometre further on you encounter the Sant Honorat monastery, with a priest at its helm today, before reaching the summit plateau of the Santuari de Nostra Senyora de Cura, founded in 1275. It was here and at Honorat that the religious philosopher, poet and missionary Ramon Llull spent ten years, laying down the foundations for his magnum opus, »Ars magna«. A statue honours the great Mallorcan, who is immortalised in stained glass and in a small museum with numerous devotional objects. Inside the monastery church is revered the early 16th century Madonna Nostra Senyora de Cura, who to the faithful is capable of healing afflictions of body and mind. The monastery, today still inhabited by Franciscan monks, has a restaurant and accommodation, simply furnished and inexpensive. The large monastery courtyard, surrounded by a low stone wall, offers views spanning the sea to the Tramuntana mountains.

Address Santuari Nostra Senyora de Cura, 07629 Randa, monastery tel. 971/660994 | Access From Palma take the Ma-15 to Algaida, then the Ma-5010 in the direction of Llucmajor | Tip A good restaurant serving Mallorcan dishes is the Es Reco de Randa at the foot of the mountain, Carrer Font 21.

88__ The Beachfront Cycle Path

Follow the water all the way to Palma

Leading from S'Arenal via Las Maravillas to Can Pastilla, the heart of the Platja de Palma, this cycle path runs immediately along the beachfront of the Bay of Palma, planted with palm trees and now almost entirely pedestrianised. Past the party zone, particularly popular with German tourists, a white sandy beach opens up, more than six kilometres / nearly 4 miles long and up to 40 metres wide, within striking distance of the area's numerous hotels. You can stop here at any time, leave the bike in the sand and jump into the water. Or take a break at one of the 15 balnearios for some liquid refreshment. Bikes can be hired from one of the many bike shops along the Platja de Palma.

Shortly beyond the seafront of Can Pastilla you will encounter a huge area with no buildings, resembling a lunar landscape. Here you pass underneath the busiest flight path approaching Palma Airport. You might like to linger a while here, as the planes come floating in above your head as if on a string of pearls, seemingly close enough to touch. Carrying on around the port of Cala Gamba, where small sailing vessels moor next to fishing boats, you'll find many picturesque bays where you can take an easy dip. Via Ciutat Jardi and the bay of Es Molinar continue on to Portixol; the city beach of Palma actually starts behind its port. Now you are cycling at an elevation along the start of the quay wall, and soon enough the Cathedral of Palma comes into view. Perfectly laid out, the cycle path then leads along the Puerto de Palma to the other end of the city and the cruise ship harbour. Always on firm concrete or tarmac, the bike path is marked in red with a white line running down the middle. Of course, you can also start this bike tour the other way round, in Palma, for a beach trip into the bay of Palma, and maybe to S'Arenal too.

Address S'Arenal–Platja de Palma–Palma and back | Access Public transport: buses no. 15, 17, 23, 31 from Palma to Platja de Palma and back | Opening times It's best to cycle in the daytime, as most rental bikes come without lights. | Tip Stop at one of the small restaurants in the harbour of the picturesque little town of El Molinar for a salad. The Puro Beach Club on a headland at the farthest end of Can Pastilla is a little more sophisticated – elegant, with white sun loungers and choice food, you can swim in the pool or sea here.

89_ The MegaPark
Brave new worlds on Platja de Palma

Although it's such a cliché, somehow you want to see it for yourself just once: Ballermann 6, Ham Street, the Beer King, and most of all, the MegaPark. You read about the masses of tourists in permanent party mode, drinking sangria from buckets through huge straws, about the big beer halls and the massive parties where apparently even the squarest guy gets a girl, where the atmosphere feels more like a football ground, and where late at night the »King of Mallorca« makes an appearance.

Sure you want to have seen all this, but without being recognised yourself or becoming associated with any of it. And so it is that many tourists roam around the block here, all the time, and all year round. A little fearful they might be, but fascinated by what goes on here. And once you stand in front of MegaPark, you just have to hand it to them: respect.

This is the most extraordinary and absurd party temple; there is simply nothing like it on the whole of Mallorca, perhaps anywhere come to that. The MegaPark comprises an entire block, directly bordering the beachfront. Make of it what you will, but spanning 8,000 square metres and rising up some 30 metres, this colossus is built like a Gothic cathedral or the ruin of an old knights' castle. Huge, colourful windows painted with massive beer jars and Bavarian lederhosen serve as a signal to passers-by, according to the managers, that »Oktoberfest« is celebrated here 180 days and nights, for the entire season.

The MegaPark »Cathedral«, with its huge MegaArena club, Mallorca's »biggest party cellar«, the gigantic beer garden with live stage or the sunken pool for foam parties, can hold up to 8,000 people with 18 bars to drink in. Depending on the season, up to 12,000 people party here every day. And a huge video screen facing the water takes the party outside as well.

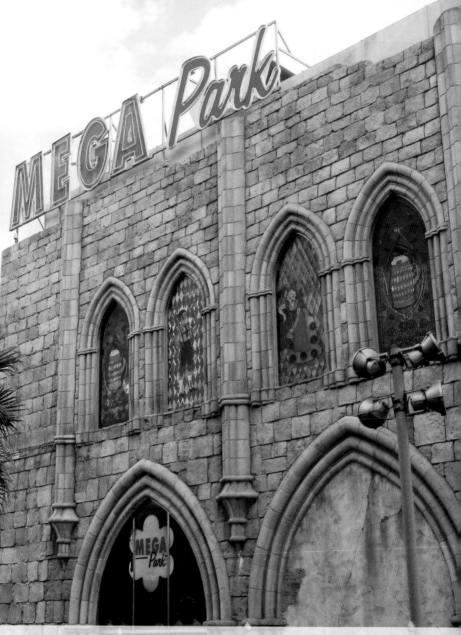

Address Carrer del Llaút 26, 07600 S'Arenal, Platja de Palma opposite the Balneario 5 | Access By car: from Palma on the Ma-19; by public transport: various buses from Palma | Opening times April–Oct daily 11am–5am | Tip Other venues for partying hard are the Riu Palace club or BCM Planet Dance across the bay in Magaluf.

90__ The Porciúncula
Modern architecture on Ham Street

There isn't much to see along the six-kilometre Platja de Palma, the stretch of coast east of Palma between Can Pastilla and S'Arenal, with its 15 so-called balnearios, apart from hotels, bars, shops, sand and beach.

Yet this corner of the island, a little off the beaten track, shelters an unusual church that's worth a second look. A church not like the various cathedrals and venerable places of worhsip in Palma – historic, sublime, full of art history treasures and buried VIPs from bygone days. No, it's a modern church, near the tourist strips of Ballermann 6 and Ham Street.

The Catholic Porciúncula, belonging to the Franciscan order, is also called the »Crystal Church«, dedicated to »Our Lady of the Angels«. Erected in 1968, the church was shaped from concrete and 600 square metres of glass, most of it colourful. Its architecture is very modern, and therefore ambitious for a Mallorcan church. The circular building, with its altar standing in the centre, is surrounded by 39 large, colourful stained-glass windows reaching up to the vaulted ceiling and representing various motifs around Saint Francis and the Creation myth. The floor is lined with marble tiles showing fish motifs.

The Crystal Church is set into the adjacent La Porciúncula park, a shady oasis of peace and calm ideal for recovering from the hectic beach life. The park was laid out as far back as 1914 by the Franciscans in the wake of their building a branch of their monastery in Palma.

Today, the Porciúncula complex also comprises a small museum with archeological ceramics and finds from the Franciscans' mission work in South America. The Porciúncula monastery also has an educational centre with a theological college, kindergarten and school.

Address La Porciúncula, Avinguda Fra. Joan Llabrés 1, 07600 S'Arenal, tel. 971/260002 | Access Public transport from Palma: bus no. 15 from Plaça de la Reina, bus no. 26 from Plaça d'Espanya, stop Porciúncula; by car: take exit 11 in Las Maravillas | Opening times June–Aug Mon–Sat 9.30am–1pm, 3.30–6.45pm; Sept–May Mon–Sat 3.30–6pm, Sun 9.30am–1pm | Tip In S'Arenal, fun lovers can take advantage of Aqualand and its collection of freshwater slides.

91__ The Sleeping Madonna

Risen from oblivion after half a century

Recently, miraculous happenings have been taking place in the Sant Crist church in the picturesque village of S'Arracó, not far from Andratx on the way to Sant Elm – events that have brought rapture and gratitude to the Catholic congregation. The current parish priest and a few of the older members of the congregation remembered that to save it from decaying, the church's recumbent Madonna had been laid in a box without much ado in the mid-1960s, and stored away in the church. Now it turns out that the Sant Crist church of S'Arracó possesses one of the very rare examples of a »Mare de Déu Morta«, known only from a few churches in Mallorca, including the cathedral in Palma and the churches of Santanyí and Valdemossa.

The reverence reserved for the »sleeping Maria« probably exists in this form only in Mallorca. On Assumption Day, around 15 August, the Madonna, usually recumbent in a side altar, is propped up in the main nave of the church and worshipped for a week. The same treatment is now afforded once more to the Madonna of S'Arracó, which dates back to the year 1528 and is considered particularly valuable in terms of art history. The Spanish sculptor and Renaissance artist Joan de Salas, renowned in his time, had created »Dormitio Mariae« for the monastery of Santa María de la Real in Palma. The Madonna only found its way to S'Arracó in 1835 in the wake of the secularisation and closure of Palma's great monasteries, when a monk took it to safety from interference and destruction.

The priest of S'Arracó has now decided to not only show the sleeping Madonna to the faithful on the day of the Assumption of Mary, but to make it accessible to anybody who is interested.

S'Arracó now has a gem worth visiting, and so the Madonna lies on a side altar in a kind of glass casket, barefoot and hands folded, clearly visible in her blue mantle with the golden aureola around her head.

Address Plaça General Weyler, 07159 S'Arracó | Access On the Ma-1030 from Andratx to Sant Elm; bus IB-35 from Andratx | Opening times irregular opening times, Sunday Mass every week at 10am | Tip The art nouveau houses near the church are impressive, and a detour to Sant Elm is worthwhile if only for the views it affords of the offshore islet of Dragonera.

92__ The Devil Masks

Strange mystical happenings in the interior

For a while now, the Museu Sant Antoni has formed part of the new museum complex of Can Planes in the heart of Sa Pobla. Not much happens here, so the staff often find themselves switching on the lights in the darkened room for visitors to start exploring tentatively the world of oversized devils and fantastical figures who await them, baring their teeth in a taunting grin, ready to strike. It all leaves quite an impression, as does watching the remarkable short film, underpinned by rousing music, which tells the story of these devils and fanciful figures when they are brought to life and set free. This happens every year during the night of the 16th to the 17th of January, when the devil really does come to town, in this case to the otherwise rather sleepy town of Sa Pobla.

This is the night of Sant Antoni, an excessive and sumptuous fiesta lasting till the early morning, and which is celebrated here as nowhere else. Demons roam the narrow lanes, frolicking red devils dancing ecstatically. There are huge masks, figures with oversized heads, the »Caparrots«, characters from folklore and the mythological monster »el Grifo«. And Saint Anthony as the central figure, plus of course the devil. There are fires everywhere, huge raging bonfires, the crackling of gigantic fireworks and the flickering tongues of flame. All accompanied by the music of the »ximbombades«, instruments made from a clay pot stretched with rabbit or goat skin, and rhythmic Mallorcan chants.

This is the night that Saint Anthony, since 1375, has fought the evil powers and temptation, scattered the demons and wintertime, and made Light victorious over Darkness. Saint Anthony is also the patron saint of cattle, which are blessed on this night, a special day in the agricultural calendar. Afterwards, the devils' costumes and bigheaded puppets are once more stowed away for another year in the Museum Sant Antoni.

Address Can Planes, Carrer Antoni Maura 6, 07420 Sa Pobla, tel. 971/542389 |
Access Public transport: by bus or train Palma−Inca−Sa Pobla; buses from Muro and
Port d'Alcúdia; by car: on the Ma-13 | Opening times Tue−Sat 10am−2pm, 4−8pm,
Sun 10am−2pm, closed Mon | Tip The Can Planes arts centre also comprises the
museum for contemporary art, the toy museum and studios for courses and seminars.

93 The Black Pigs
Meet the porcine residents of Els Calderers

In contrast to the neighbouring towns of Petra and Sineu and their great cultural treasures, Sant Joan is all about sausages.

Agriculture dominates here, and Sant Joan is the birthplace of the famous »botifarrónes« blood pudding and the »sobrasada de Mallorca«, a speciality sausage unique to the island, whose geographical origin enjoys European projection and which may only be produced here. The sobrasada is a sausage made from the black pig or »porc negre«, a special porcine breed traditionally only bred in Mallorca.

And the sausage has to be produced according to a very special recipe with strictly limited ingredients. Sant Joan and its surroundings form the stronghold of pig breeding and the sausage factories, of which there are around a dozen.

Those who would like to meet the black pig should head for the Els Calderers country estate a little outside Sant Joan below the Puig de Bonany hermitage, which can trace its history back to the 13th century.

The baronial manor as you see it today, open to the public since the mid-1990s, was built in 1750 and belonged to the blue-blooded Verí family, who continually had it extended.

Alongside the impressive and lavishly furnished manor house that takes visitors back in time 200 years, numerous additional buildings form part of Els Calderers: a large Mallorcan kitchen for the staff, the larder and various workshops with their historic machinery, a chapel, the wine cellar. Everything seems as if the estate had only been left yesterday, and its inhabitants might come back any minute.

However, the only real life here goes on in the numerous stables, where the famous black pigs are amongst the livestock being bred.

Address Els Calderers, 07240 Sant Joan, tel. 971/526069 | Access Ma-15 Carretera Palma–Manacor, exit (signposted) at km 37 | Opening times April–Oct 10am–6pm, Nov–March 10am–5pm | Tip Shortly before reaching Sant Joan you will see the small 13th century church of Santuari de la Mare Déu de Consolació, freshly renovated.

94__ The Jewish Cemetery

A reminder of the hard times suffered by Mallorca's Jews

In 1978 Mallorca's Jewish community, today comprising around 200 families, laid out their cemetery in Santa Eugènia, traditionally a centre of Jewish life on the island. Mallorca's only Jewish cemetery enjoys a thoroughly peaceful location behind a cast-iron gate with Hebrew lettering, immediately behind the town's communal cemetery.

There has been a large Jewish community on Mallorca for centuries. However, following the Reconquista from the mid-12th century, it was increasingly subject to large-scale persecution. In the Middle Ages, four synagogues in Palma represented the Jewish community, which played a prominent role in the money-lending business and gold and silver trade – with the consequence that many Christians were heavily indebted to Jews. From 1300 tensions escalated, with pogroms breaking out repeatedly, despite Jews being tolerated by the King and accorded privileges. In the early 15th century, the Jewish community comprised over 1,000 families. But in 1435, disaster struck. Hundreds of Jews were killed, many were forced to convert to Christianity, yet stayed as »secret Jews« or »Xuetes«. Once the Inquisition had done its work, there were hardly any Jews left on Mallorca. However, the Xuetes too always remained victims of persecutions.

From 1933 onwards, many German Jews emigrated to Mallorca, hoping to find a safe haven. However, the Nazis who had lived here since the Spanish Civil War, former members of the »Legion Condor«, were active as spies for Germany. In mid-1940, Hitler demanded of the Spanish dictator General Franco that Mallorca be »free of Jews« – in short, that they be deported. For most of them this spelled certain death. The Jews that had been converted by force in the Middle Ages were also included in this demand, which the Spanish did however resist. It wasn't until 1971 that the first Jewish community since 1435 settled once more on Mallorca.

ישראל עד יקיץ וייחשך שוכבי עפר

Address Camí de Muntanya, 07142 Santa Eugènia, Jewish congregation: Comunidad Judaía de Mallorca, Carrer de Monsenyor Palmer 3, 07014 Palma, tel. 971/283799 | Access From Palma take the Ma-3011 in the direction of Sineu, exit onto the Ma-3040 | Opening times The cemetery is usually locked, but you can get a good idea by looking through the cast-iron gate. | Tip A short walk through Santa Eugènia reveals two splendid windmills.

זך ישר בתום לבבך בשמת מרה
לזכרון עולם ולאשרי בשמת שרת
בתיה כרבלה בת בניסין קרין לנדאוי ע"ה
יצחק בן מר ה שלמה הכריך ע"ה
ידעת כל הבריות
מתעיר קראדא - מליציה
ת.נ.צ.ב.ה.

95__ The Wine Express
A train journey through the heart of winemaking

It was the Romans who brought wine to Mallorca, and in the Middle Ages the wine trade blossomed to the extent that the majority of rural jobs were in viticulture. In the 19th century Mallorcan wine, the sweetish Malvasía grape in particular, experienced a real boom, and dessert wines from Mallorca became a hit on the Spanish mainland too.

Until, that is, around 1900, when the phylloxera bug came to the island, annihilating the vineyards of the Pla and those on the high plain towards the Tramuntana mountains. Viniculture on Mallorca stopped almost entirely, and it took a long time for the island to recover.

Now, since the 1980s, winemaking has been restarted intensively and on a large scale, with the recultivation of vineyards and old wineries brought back to life. The idea was to reconnect with the centuries-old tradition of Mallorcan wine culture. Today, Mallorca's wines are once more a fixture on the wine circuit, with the ones produced around Binissalem of a particularly high quality. And so it is that in this region you will find, in the Ferrer and Macià Batle wine estates, two of the largest wineries on the island, both in private hands. Alongside them you have many smaller estates, of no less a standard, producing both white and red wines. The Mediterranean climate ensures quality.

These days you can explore the vineyards of the Binissalem area twice a day aboard a little train, the »Mallorca Wine Express«, trundling through fields and vineyards, learning all about wine and grape cultivation, watching the vintners at work, and of course sampling some of the good stuff and stocking up on a few bottles. The train takes two hours for the leisurely trip, starting from the Macià Batle estate, and calling at various wineries, amongst them Can Rubí, Vins Nadal and Ribas.

Address Camí de Coanegra, 07320 Santa Maria del Camí, mobile tel. 653528659 or 971/140014 (Macià Batle) | Access Ma-13 from Palma to Alcúdia, exit Santa Maria del Camí, by train from Palma to Inca or from Manacor via Inca to Palma | Opening times The best way to enquire about the tour timetables is to phone the tourist information. | Tip Don't miss the guided tour through the Bodega Macià Batle, one of the largest on Mallorca, with winetasting and snacks, tel. 971/140014.

96__The Stone Cross

Where King Jaume I landed to defeat the Arabs

Far from all the tourist mayhem and the seemingly uncontrollable building boom around the rocky bay of Santa Ponça with its sandy beach, you can discover a monument that gives a deep insight into the history of the island. It was right here, where the large white cross stands resplendent and visible from afar, that a part of Mallorca's medieval history began, one which has important repercussions to this day. It was in the bay of Santa Ponça, immediately next to where the chic marina and the Club Nàutic are today, that on 12 September 1229 the troops of Jaume I of Aragón landed to reconquer the island for Christendom and to banish the Muslim Moors who had ruled for three centuries. Here, at the end of the small peninsula of Sa Caleta, is where the Reconquista, the bloody fight for Mallorca, started. The Arab troops were defeated and Palma eventually taken.

The white stone cross, the Cruz de la Conquista, was built in 1929 to commemorate the 700th anniversary of the landing of the King, his 150 ships and fighting force of 15,000 men. This is where the first royal flag is said to have been hoisted. The eight stone reliefs on the pedestal of the cross represent various events during the reconquest of Mallorca, including the celebration of the first Holy Mass on Mallorcan soil. Today, the Capilla de la Piedra Sagrada or »Chapel of the Holy Stone« in Palma's city centre still safeguards a large block of stone as a relic; it is said that the first Mass following the landing of the King and his troops was celebrated on this very rock.

Since then, every first weekend in September the invasion of 1229 is staged as part of the Moros i Cristians festival. The landing of the Christian ships, the first battles between Moors and Christians and the successful re-Christianisation are re-enacted, complete with a great big fiesta.

Address Via de la Creu, 07180 Santa Ponça | Access Take the Ma-1 from Palma to Andratx, exit Ma-1013 for Santa Ponça, then take the Via de la Creu to Sa Caleta and the marina | Tip Recommended alternatives to the beach of Santa Ponça, which can get very busy, are the beaches of Portals Vells above the Cap de Cala Figuera.

97__ The Flor de Sal Shop
Harvesting and selling the best salt

You won't believe how many types of salt there are. And the ones from Mallorca, from the salt works on Es Trenc to be precise, actually rank among the best of their kind. The idea to develop it beyond purely a cooking salt started in early 2000 with a young Swiss entrepreneur.

Securing access to the salt works between the Colònia de Sant Jordi and the dune beach of Es Trenc, she turned the Flor de Sal into a successful brand – with a little shop in the salt works and one in Santanyí. The factory of this small-scale company, employing just ten people, is right nearby.

Flor de Sal d'Es Trenc is a pure, entirely natural product with an extraordinarily high mineral and magnesium content, and an excellent taste to boot. The ideal conditions are here: crystal-clear sea water and a constant breeze.

When sun and air evaporate the water caught in the salt basins, the snow-white crystals remain. The top layer of these fine salt crystals is skimmed off by hand, using special hooks, »harvested« and dried. Flor de Sal is available as pure sea salt, or in a more sophisticated version with herbs and spices produced in Santanyí, resulting in special and unusual flavour variations.

Salt harvesting has been a part of Mallorca seemingly forever. The Phoenicians extracted their salt in the nearby salt works of Llevant, as did the Romans and Arabs who followed them.

A brisk commercial trade in salt has taken place here since the 13th century, always using the same traditional extraction method. Salt has been harvested in the Es Trenc works since the mid-20th century.

Today, the Flor de Sal from Es Trenc has become a great success. It is sold in gourmet shops and is popular not only with top chefs, but also with an increasing number of private gastronomers.

Address Carrer Asprer 11, 07650 Santanyí, tel. 971/653385 | Access Ma-19 motorway Palma–Llucmajor, continuing on the Carretera via Campos to Santanyí | Opening times in summer daily 9.30am–2pm and 5–8pm, in winter 10am–2pm | Tip The salt works and small shop lie on the Carretera Campos–Colònia de Sant Jordí, km 10, where the extension of the side street leads to the car park of Es Trenc beach.

98__ The Organ of Jordi Bosch

Heavenly sounds in the church of Sant Andreu

The organ of Sant Andreu church in Santanyí is considered the finest on the island, its sound acclaimed as divine and not of this world. Organists who have played here sing its praises as much as the organ builders who have tried to emulate it and the audience members who have heard many concerts on different organs. However, the organ at Sant Andreu, an 18th century church standing on Plaça Major in Santanyí, is very much of this world, being the masterpiece of the highly talented and musically well-versed Mallorcan organ builder Jordi Bosch (1736–1800), whose fame and glory soon extended beyond Mallorca's borders, setting him on the path to becoming royal organ builder. The Santanyí organ of 1762 was his first really major piece of work, the one which was to prove his exceptional talent in this highly skilled profession.

At the time, Jordi Bosch, who hailed from an organ-building family and would go on to build the organ of the cathedral of Seville, as well as the one in Madrid's royal palace, was only 26 years old.

In actual fact, Bosch built the organ for the monastery of Santo Domingo in Palma. However, after the closure of the Dominican monastery in 1837, it was sold to Santanyí and put in storage. It was only 50 years later that the organ was reactivated, initially in a toned-down version with fewer manuals.

However, the complex instrument needed frequent repairs and constant, thorough maintenance. In 1984, the organ was restored by renowned German organ builder Gerhard Grenzing in order to realise its full potential. Today, the organ shines as a visual highlight, but most of all it is the unique sound quality which fills the furthest corners of the church. Its unique trompeteria in particular provides the bright triumphal sound that Jordi Bosch gave it 250 years ago.

Address Plaça Major 31, 07650 Santanyí, Tel. 971/653152 | Access Ma-19 motorway
Palma–Llucmajor, then continue on the Carretera via Campos to Santanyí | Opening
times The church is sometimes open in the daytime. Occasional organ concerts are held
in Sant Andreu. | Tip Also worth seeing is the 14th century predecessor to Sant Andreu
church, the Capella de Roser (adjacent to and connected with Sant Andreu).

99__ The Stone Horses

The extraordinary sculptures of Rolf Schaffner

There is a hidden gem in Santanyí. Unearthing this treasure is not so easy, but once you've discovered it you will not cease to be amazed. Taking the road south to Es Llombards you pass the roundabout with the »Rey y Reina« sculpture. To your left is a rather wild, overgrown tract of land. Battle your way through the thick scrub for a few yards and suddenly they emerge in front of you: the »Caballos«, seven huge horses of layered natural stone. This proud herd has been standing here since 1963, when the German artist and sculptor Rolf Schaffner (1927–2008), who spent over four decades living and making art in Santanyí, created this unusual sculpture, which nature has now enfolded in its embrace.

But that's not all. Taking the road from Santanyí to Campos, after about three kilometres and just before reaching the village of Son Danusset, on your left you'll find, equally obscured from view, an impossible-seeming group of sculptures.

At first glance it feels as if you've stepped back into a prehistoric era or the Aztec culture of Central America. A pile of monumental stone blocks, up to six metres high, stands between the almond and olive trees, surrounded by dense undergrowth. This is »Son Danús«, the open-air plot that served Rolf Schaffner as both studio and exhibition space. (Visits can be arranged through the Flohr Gallery in Santanyí, tel. 690218709.)

The sculptor's material of choice was always the yellowy-reddish stones, his inspiration the many different stone buildings on Mallorca and the commonly-used drystone method, spanning the island's history. Schaffner's ingenious stone stacks and the way he shaped them defy clear categorisation, shifting between Land Art and abstract sculpture, between archaic and contemporary. The aforementioned »Rey y Reina« on the roundabout at Santanyí is another work by the same artist.

Address 07650 Santanyí | Access Take the road from Santanyí to Campos, km 47 (Sculpture Park) | Tip The oversized sculpture on Cala Santanyí near the Es Pontas rock is one of Schaffner's last works, forming the southernmost point of his international sculpture project »Equilibrio« (»Meridians of Peace«) at five sites in Europe.

100__ The Bunker of Es Trenc

Pieces of history on an idyllic beach

Many Mallorcan insiders consider the beach of Es Trenc, some five kilometres / three miles long between Ses Covetes and Colònia de Sant Jordi, the finest stretch of coast on the island. It is certainly the longest on Mallorca that is not built up. Its fans rave about the fine white sand, the adjacent dunes covered with bizarre beach grass, and the many pine forests. The beach enjoys protected status for a few miles inland as well, sparing it from land speculation and the construction boom, even if Ses Covetes, the village you encounter first at Es Trenc, displays numerous illegally built summer houses, whose proliferation has been stopped but which to this day haven't been torn down. Unfinished, abandoned constructions sit right by the sea alongside restaurants, beach shacks and a clutch of legal residences.

Ruins of a very different kind might surprise you during a walk along the beach. Between the waterline and the banked-up dunes you'll encounter large old bunkers, cubes cast from concrete with massive walls, seemingly impregnable. Two narrow vertical slits show where the machine guns would have poked out to open fire on enemy ships or soldiers attempting to land.

Today, tourists occasionally seek shelter from the sun in the shade of the concrete, while others sunbathe naked nearby, as parts of this beach are nudist.

But few know the story behind these bunkers, when and why these colossal absurdities came to be on this protected beach. In fact, the bunkers were built between 1940 and 1950 because the fascist Franco dictatorship was constantly worried that the victorious allies, who had vanquished fascism in Germany and Italy, would also take Spain in their sights in order to exact vengeance, not least for the regime's role in the Spanish Civil War (1936–1939), when the Republic was violently hijacked.

Address Platja Es Trenc, 07639 Ses Covetes or 07638 Colònia de Sant Jordi | Access
Either take the access road to the Es Trenc beach along the road from Campos to Colònia
Sant Jordi, or from Campos in the direction of Sa Ràpita via the Ses Covetes access road |
Tip On the way to Colonia de Sant Jordi there is another road to Es Trenc, running behind
the salt works, with a large car park in front of the dunes. To the east of Ses Covetes, you
hit the Platja de Sa Ràpita, a beach quite similar to Es Trenc and also protected.

101__ The Cactus Farm
At Toni Moreno's they come in all sizes

There is a bit of the Arizona or New Mexico desert vibe when you observe these extensive fields of cacti behind the inviting finca and the large greenhouses. The backdrop to a spaghetti western by Warner Bros or MGM perhaps. Certainly you seem to have left the sunny island of Mallorca far behind, with its lush landscape usually dominated by palm, olive and almond trees, citrus fruit and winemaking, fertile valleys and countless streams. Toni Moreno's finca on the edge of the town of Ses Salines, with its cacti as far as the eye can see, is unique on Mallorca.

The best way to approach Toni and the unusual World of Cacti in his nursery, at the end of Carrer Einstein, is from the village proper. Here too you will find huge glasshouses and open spaces with thousands of spiky specimens.

You can buy cacti and, if you wish, get an introduction to the world of these curious plants.

The Morenos grow some 500 species of cacti across 40,000 square metres, from huge statuesque examples down to those that will fit your window sill back home. When Toni Moreno started cultivating cacti in 1972, he was still focusing on the smaller kinds. However, once his daughter Antonia – who had studied in California, discovering the vast variety of the species – came on board too, there was no holding back. From then on the monster cacti were grown here too.

Today, the Morenos are one of the largest Spanish cacti farms and have an international client base, delivering all the way to China. Ordering is done online and the goods are shipped in containers. Every year, the small family firm with its four employees sells between 20,000 and 25,000 cacti. The larger specimens are not exactly cheap, but this is because cacti grow very slowly and like to be treated well.

Address Cactus Toni Moreno, Carrer Einstein, 07640 Ses Salines, tel. 971/649280 |
Access Coming from Campos on the Ma-6040/Ma-6101 or from Santanyí on the
Ma-6100 to Ses Salines. The Carrer Einstein leads from Campos at the entrance to the
village off the Ma-6100 – continue to its end. | Opening times Mon–Fri 8am–1pm and
3–6pm| Tip Close to Ses Salines on the Ma-6100 you can discover the »Botanicactus«
botanical gardens, which holds a huge cacti garden alongside many other plants.

102__ The Winged Lion

A market under constant supervision

With a centuries-old tradition, Sineu's Wednesday market is considered the best in Mallorca. This is due to the quality of the wares for sale here, and the variety of produce. After all, the small hillside town of Sineu represents the geographic centre of the island, the agricultural hub of the fertile Es Pla plain.

On the central Plaça d'Espanya, but also in the numerous little side alleys and on the steps and terraces of the picturesque medieval town, fruit and veg are sold alongside all kinds of olives, spices, fish and meat, mostly at good prices. This is where the Mallorcans come to buy.

Tourists are drawn to the several stalls that offer crafts, fabrics, leather goods and ceramics, but agricultural tools are for sale too, and you will see knife grinders and potters at work.

Of particular interest is the cattle market of Sineu, the only one of its kind in Mallorca, on the Plaça del Fossar. There is a lot of traditional-style loud haggling here, until the deal is sealed with a handshake.

Some farmers load their purchases onto cattle trucks, while others leave the market with chickens and ducks under their arms. Many will first celebrate a successful sale by heading to one of the bars and cellars surrounding the market, which are full to bursting point on market day.

And supervising the whole market business is the Lion of Sineu. Sure of himself and his victory, the bronze Lleó de Sant Marc occupies this prominent position here in honour of Mark the Evangelist, the town's patron saint.

The winged lion has been watching over the market and its people in front of the town's most important church, the 13th-century Nostra Senyora dels Àngels with its mighty free-standing 16th century bell tower, since 1945.

Address Plaça d'Espanya, 07510 Sineu | Access Take the Ma-3011 from Palma or the Ma-3320/Ma-3300 from Manacor via Petra | Opening times The market is held every Wednesday morning. | Tip The Convento de Monjas monastery in Carrer Arnoldo Ramis, a former palace of Jaume II, is worth seeing, as is the art gallery in the art nouveau former train station in Carrer S'Estació.

103__ The Can Prunera Museum

A rival to the Es Baluard in the Tramuntana mountains

Everything fits together here in this narrow street in the heart of Sóller: the interior of this fine museum of modern art and the art nouveau villa built by a local entrepreneur in 1911. It was created at a time when the wealthy citizens of the town, having made their fortunes abroad, had returned and were competing to own the most beautiful house in Sóller. Now this splendid villa, with its impressive facade and artistic reliefs, stands so high up on this narrow street that you have to strain your neck to take it all in. And the house has a lot to offer visually – the colourful ornate glass windows, the tiled floor, the curved staircase, the painstakingly restored furniture. From the cellar up to the attic everything is the finest art nouveau, down to the last detail, and all original. And since 2009 the place has been home to one of the most beautiful museums on the island.

The various rooms of Can Prunera display art nouveau objects by local and international artists of the Spanish modernismo, Joan Miró's book illustrations, an important collection of antique dolls and high-calibre exhibits of modern art by Picasso, Miró, Magritte, Léger, Barceló and Nolde. There are also selected works by Jordi Rames, one of the most important Mallorcan artists of the first half of the 20th century, while the charmingly laid-out garden contains a dozen unusual sculptures.

Around two thirds of these paintings and objects come from the Serra Collection, and until recently could be seen in the Es Baluard Museum in Palma, sponsored by Pedro Serra. However, the prominent patron of the arts and influential publisher of the Serra media group withdrew some of his loans, and these he now displays at Can Prunera, belonging to the Fundació Tren de l'Art, which Serra helped to set up.

Address Carrer de Sa Lluna 86 and 90, 07100 Sóller, tel. 971/638973, www.canprunera.com | Access Coming from the station (Estació del Tren de Sóller) via Plaça d'Espanya and Plaça Sa Constitució into Carrer de la Lluna | Opening times daily 10.30am–6.30pm, Oct–March closed Mon | Tip The centre of Sóller has more examples of the finest art nouveau architecture, the Sant Bartolomé church in particular.

104__ The Historic Tram

A trundle through town

There is only one tram on the Balearics, and that's the one running from Sóller four kilometres / 2.5 miles north to Port de Sóller, where eventually it reaches its destination at the harbour promenade. It is exactly this little electric tram that was introduced after the opening of the Palma – Sóller train route and inaugurated in 1913. Also run by the Ferrocarril de Sóller, it has brought new life to the horseshoe-shaped harbour, from which the town's 2,500 inhabitants benefit twice over. The majority of tourists come in the daytime to visit the promenade and restaurants, and depart again in the evenings, leaving the port to fall back into its old slow pace of life and Port de Sóller to become once again a fishing village.

The Tranvía de Sóller is an attraction well worth taking advantage of, if only for a gentle meander to the harbour. Everything is as it was 100 years ago, when it would head towards the coast with its old engine and wooden carriages, open to the elements, past orchards and orange groves laden with fruit. At the time, the tram would also transport goods alongside passengers, including fresh fish. Today, it runs every half hour in the summer, taking around 20 minutes and stopping about a dozen times. The point of departure is the train station in the heart of Sóller, a converted town palace dating back to the 17th century, which had numerous art nouveau elements added to it later. The tracks are connected to the exit by an imposing staircase. And last but not least, the station shelters – and this could be unique worldwide – a museum of the Tren de l'Art foundation promoting modern art, where you can admire Mirós and Picassos right by the train tracks. From here, the route runs right across the Plaça de la Constitució, the town's central square, past the 13th-century Sant Bartolomeu church and through the many street cafés under the shady plane trees. Occasionally customers have to push their chairs back a little so the tram can pass.

Address Plaça d'Espanya 6, 07100 Sóller, tel. 971/630130 | Access from Palma to Sóller via the Ma-11 | Opening times In summer, the tram runs every half-hour, in winter every hour. | Tip A handy detour from Sóller runs to the picturesque village of Fornalutx.

105__ The Beach of Dunes

Peace and quiet away from the large resorts

If it wasn't for the mountains you might think you were on England's north Norfolk coast. Mallorca has no shortage of beautiful sandy beaches and picturesque coves, but a dune landscape such as the one at Son Serra de Marina is harder to find.

This protected beach, some 1.5 km long with the odd small pine forest and dunes reaching far inland, starts on the eastern edge of the little town, right behind the Torrent de na Borges. And it isn't full of tourists; in fact, out of season there's hardly anybody here. You can walk far beyond the obelisk standing in the dunes, and it's hard to believe you're still on Mallorca. There's no beach lounge, no snack bar, and that is its charm – just bring your own picnic and enjoy a completely different experience.

The only appeal of the small town of Son Serra de Marina – purely a holiday place, designed on the architect's drawing board and placed in to the landscape – lies in the fact that all the houses keep to a similar height and there is a lack of large resorts. Most are holiday homes in private hands, and every street in town leads directly to the sea.

In summer the place has around 1,000 inhabitants, but out of season Son Serra de Marina resembles a ghost town and you're lucky to find anybody around.

Few residents spend the winter here, although some come down at weekends to check that everything is shipshape. Yet, even in summer, Son Serra de Marina doesn't get uncomfortable. The beaches are not overrun, in sharp contrast to nearby Can Picafort. The facilities are accordingly sparse, with a supermarket, pharmacy, bakery and a handful of restaurants, as well as a small marina for pleasure boats and yachts.

Address Platja de sa Canova, 07450 Son Serra de Marina | Access Ma-12 Alcúdia via Can Picafort to Artà, exit Son Serra de Marina, buses from Can Picafort. Parking is available at the eastern end of town, right by the start of the beach. | Tip To reach another dune beach, only accessible on foot, head west to the Platja de Son Real in the direction of Son Bauló. At the beginning of the Platja de sa Canova, the Sunshine-Bar El Sol, a beach bar/restaurant with a Caribbean vibe, remains open in winter.

106__ The Església Nova Church

Today, the Unfinished One serves an an open-air stage

This is truly unique in Mallorca. A roofless church with open windows, yet still worthy of architectural accolades; a mighty facade with a daring curve, in the heart of the city but barely visible from the street. This is the Església Nova, the new unfinished church in Son Servera, this charming little town near the east coast of the island, which was so heavily fought over during the Spanish Civil War.

In 1905, Catalan architect Joan Rubió i Bellver (1870–1952) was given the commission to erect another church next to the Sant Joan Bautista parish church, which had stood there since the 18th century. A close collaborator of Antoni Gaudí (1852–1926), the architect started work on a church in the neo-Gothic style.

What you see today is a nave of strict simplicity, mighty church windows, lancet arches and rosettes, but all open to the heavens. And why is this? Simply that the building owners ran out of money. Work on the church continued until 1929, when the plug was finally pulled on the project. So today the church stands there, for some a ruin, for others a modern building, avant garde even.

Here in Son Servera, people have grown accustomed to this state of affairs, and all initiatives to perhaps complete the church after all are met with consistent refusal. After all, it would lose its uniqueness, its fascination, and become just one more church amongst many.

After extensive renovation and restoration works in the mid-1990s and again in 2007/2008, today the unfinished church is mainly given over to cultural events, from open-air concerts to traditional Mallorcan folk dance in summer, along with the occasional religious ceremony. For these, chairs are placed on the large lawn and the »Unfinished One« is simply turned into an open-air stage.

Address Plaça de Sant Ignasi, 07550 Son Servera, information city hall tel. 971/567002 | Access from Palma on the Ma-15 in the direction of Manacor to Sant Llorenc des Cardassar, then on the Ma-4030 to Son Servera | Opening times always open in the daytime, and most evenings | Tip The big attraction of this small town is the weekly market on the central Plaça de Sant Joan, taking place on a Friday.

107__The Reservoir Lakes

*Cúber and Gorg Blau: supplying Mallorca's
drinking water*

Up here on Puig Major, at 1445 metres/4740 feet the mightiest peak in the Tramuntana range, you will find two large lakes. Cúber and Gorg Blau sit in the landscape as if they had been here for millions of years.

However, these lakes – the smaller Cúber a couple of miles above the larger Gorg Blau – are entirely man-made. In the 1970s, following decades of planning, the valleys were dammed and flooded, in order to ensure the drinking-water supply to the city of Palma. For in the wake of the tourist boom, the big city had been struggling with water shortages in the summer months, just like other areas of Mallorca.

The picturesquely situated lakes are fed by numerous streams from the Tramuntana Mountains, particularly from Puig Major, in addition to the often heavy rainfalls in autumn and winter, as well as the annual snowmelt. The two lakes are connected to each other, so if Gorg Blau is holding too much water, it can flow into Cúber. The clear mountain water reaches Palma via a complex system of water pipes and tunnels. In the summer months, when too much water is being used for tourism and, more recently, for the running of the numerous golf courses and spas, water levels go down accordingly.

The atmosphere up here at the two lakes provides a real contrast to beach and sea. Amidst mighty rock formations, small holm oak forests and lush vegetation at the water's edge, you are surrounded by perfect stillness.

The GR 221 long-distance trail passes both lakes, and it's possible to leave the car behind and approach the lakes independently. A small wooden gate takes you to the shore of the Cúber, and it will take around an hour and a half to walk once around Gorg Blau, although sturdy footwear is required.

Address 07315 Son Torrella (Escorca) | **Access** The reservoir lakes are reached by the Ma-10 from Sóller via Fornalutx to Son Torella or from Pollença via Lluc. | **Tip** The solidly built brick snow houses, for the collection and storage of snow and the production of ice along the Ses Voltes d'en Galileu trail from Cúber to the Lluc Monastery in the Tramuntana Mountains, are an added attraction. The Cases de Neu were abandoned with the introduction of electric freezing facilities (there are ruins of snowhouses along the GR 221 long-distance trail).

108__ The Catalina Tiles

A reminder of Catalina Tomàs on almost every house

In Valldemossa, you will encounter Catalina Tomàs wherever you go. The patron saint of the town is omnipresent, even if no one can say for sure exactly what she did. Some say she had visions, others that she experienced religious ecstasies, and she is also said to have worked several miracles.

Having erected an altar outside the town gates, she could be found there praying incessantly. In any case, she had an engaging spirit and led a life of deep piety, which quickly became known around town.

Catalina Tomàs was born in 1531, the daughter of a farmer in Carrer Rectoria 5. Today, the small house has been converted into a chapel that is usually open. The way to the chapel leads through the beautifully laid-out leafy lanes of the lower village. At the age of 21, Catalina Tomàs joined the Augustinian convent of Santa Maria Magdalena in Palma, where she lived until her death in 1574. Her body is laid out in a glass casket in the convent church of Santa Maria Magdalena.

Revered long after her death, she was beatified as early as 1792, but only canonised in 1930 by Pope Pius XI. Today, she is the only Catholic saint from Mallorca.

In honour of »La Beata«, as she is called in Valldemossa, a great procession is held on 28 July, the Carro Triomfal, with a six-year old girl representing Saint Catalina.

You will find colourful tiles on houses all over town depicting episodes from the life of Catalina Tomàs, examples of her good works, and fanciful legends. Her monument stands in front of the Gothic parish church of Valldemossa, which holds the certificate of her beatification. Catalina is also immortalised on an image high above the altar in the church of the former Carthusian charterhouse.

Address Carrer Rectoria 5, 07170 Valldemossa | **Access** from Palma on the Ma-1110 | **Opening times** In the daytime, the chapel is always open. | **Tip** For those who fancy staying the night in the heart of the Old Town, the extravagant »Es Petit Hotel« is recommended, Carrer Uetam, tel. 971/612479.

SANTA CATALINA THOMAS PREGAU PER NOSALTRES

109__The Chopin Piano
The true instrument of the genius composer

As you step inside the walls of the former Carthusian monastery of Valldemossa, it's easy to imagine how cold, clammy and uncomfortable it might get in winter. You can only assume that the air here must have been sheer poison for the pneumonic Frédéric Chopin. Initially the composer didn't even have his own piano – having sent for it from Paris it was confiscated by customs. So the man who composed to survive was forced to put his masterpieces to paper using a borrowed, out-of-tune instrument. And when the 26-year old Chopin strolled through the village with his life partner, French writer George Sand, ten years his senior, and their two children, the people kept a distrustful distance.

The artistic couple didn't last even two months here, even the beauty of the landscape and the healthy climate couldn't compensate for conditions during the six weeks of the winter of 1838/39 which seemed to be never-ending. This is where Chopin composed his raindrop prelude, while Sand was to immortalise their stay in her bestseller »A Winter in Mallorca«. For the hitherto sleepy Valldemossa, however, the unbidden guests turned out to be a stroke of good fortune. The former monk's cells 2 and 4, where the romantic pair worked and lived with the children, became a tourist attraction, the piano left behind by the genius composer when they left drawing music lovers like a magnet.

But which piano was his? For decades, legions of visitors and Chopin lovers have been worshipping the wrong instrument. The rooms of the charterhouse, which was privatised in the wake of secularisation in 1835, used to belong to different families who rented the converted rooms out to the artists and are still their owners today. It was only in 2011 that the courts decided that the »Pleyel«-brand piano currently on display is indeed the instrument on which Chopin composed his immortal music.

Address Sa Cartoixa, Plaça de la Cartoixa 11, 07170 Valldemossa, tel. 971/612106 | Access from Palma take the Ma-1110 | Opening times April–Sept Mon–Sat 9.30am–6pm, Sun 10am–1pm; Feb/March, Oct/Nov Mon–Sat 9.30am–5pm, Sun 10am–1pm; Dec Mon–Sat 9.30am–3pm, concerts several times a day between 10.30am and 6pm | Tip In the charterhouse the old monastic pharmacy, which remained open to the villagers up to 1913, a valuable library and the 15th-century printing press are highly recommended, as is a visit to the monastery church and the museum.

110__ The Nixe

Michael Douglas honours the archduke
in the Costa Nord

The Tramuntana range enthralled Hollywood star Michael Douglas the moment he stepped on Mallorcan soil. The mountains, the sea, the wild coast. And the other reason he loves Mallorca is that here he can spend his holidays in relative peace and quiet, without being bothered too much. Of course, the film star didn't just buy any old finca, but one with a most distinguished history. The »S'Estaca« manor near Valldemossa was built by the Austrian Archduke Ludwig, or Luis, Salvator, for Catalina Homar, his lover and the mother of his children, the daughter of a Mallorcan carpenter who also managed his vineyards. The archduke first came to Mallorca in 1867 and fell in love with the place permanently. In turn, Michael Douglas was fascinated – from his first stay on Mallorca – by the archduke, this noble aesthete, researcher, humanist and friend of sensual delights. Which is why he placed the archduke at the centre of the Costa Nord arts centre that he founded and set up, giving him new life. The Costa Nord is now part of the environmental foundation of the island of Mallorca, but Michael Douglas has not relinquished his responsibilities.

So it is that visitors to Costa Nord meet the »Nixe«, the legendary steam-yacht with which the archduke and his crew, usually many people, crisscrossed the Mediterranean, exploring as far afield as America when it wasn't anchored off Son Marroig. Here in Costa Nord, parts of the »Nixe« have been recreated in a multimedia presentation, allowing visitors to look inside the boat and go on a virtual journey with the archduke.

Alongside the »Nixe«, the Costa Nord shows an impressive film on the Tramuntana coast and the northwest of Mallorca, full of cinematic highlights and with a grandiose soundtrack, all presented by the man himself, Michael Douglas.

Puig d'es Boixos

Cap de Tramuntana

Es Tossals Verds

Address Centro Cultural Costa Nord, Avinguda Palma 6, 07170 Valldemossa,
tel. 971/612425 | **Access** from Palma on the Ma-1110 | **Opening times** daily 9am–5pm |
Tip In summer there are regular concerts in the open-air cinema of the Costa Nord, which
is turned into a small theatre for the occasion.

La Granja

Mola de s'Esclop

111 Roundabout Art

Mallorca's roundabouts are becoming increasingly eye-catching

Art on roundabouts is in at the moment, and this applies to Mallorca too. Actually, in a very impressive way here, as there can hardly be a single roundabout on the island that hasn't been given some kind of original artistic treatment. Roundabouts are an effective means of displaying art in an enduring way and visible to anybody willing to consume it on a drive-by basis, as it were. You get to see art that is abstract or more realistic, scenes from daily life, fine detail or bombastic installations. And if you really like the look of one of the works, why not drive round the roundabout a few more times at leisure before taking your exit.

The creators of these artworks are not easy to identify, as the roundabouts offer no clue as to who is behind the individual installations. Of course, driving by wouldn't really allow much reading anyway. This would make it even more interesting to have a list of the roundabouts, as many of these artworks are much more than just some decorative item placed on the untouched centre.

One roundabout on the Ma-15 from Palma to Manacor particularly catches the eye. At Vilafranca de Bonany, at the turn-offs to Petra and Felanitx, you will suddenly be confronted with oversized people milled from steel, men and women moving in formation with uplifted hands as if in a ballet, each with two faces, some of them painted, placed opposite each other in different bearings yet creating a harmonious ensemble. This captivating installation is called »Ball de Cultures« and was created in 2005 by Miguel Sarasate, who was born in 1952 in Zaragoza and has lived and worked in Artà since 1970. And the island has more of his art in the public realm. One such piece is the »Pins de Son Servera« roundabout created in 2008 at the exit of Son Servera town – trees made from steel with overhead wires as part of an ecological street project.

Address Ma-15 Rotonda Petra/Felanitx, 07250 Vilafranca de Bonany | Access on the
Ma-15 between Vilafranca de Bonany and Manacor | Tip If you fancy taking a break
right by the »Ball de Cultures« roundabout, try some lunch in the Mallorcan restaurant
»Es Cruce«.

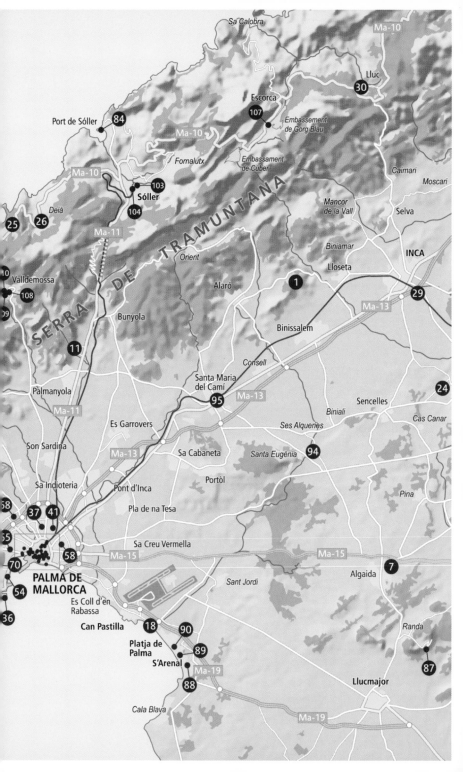

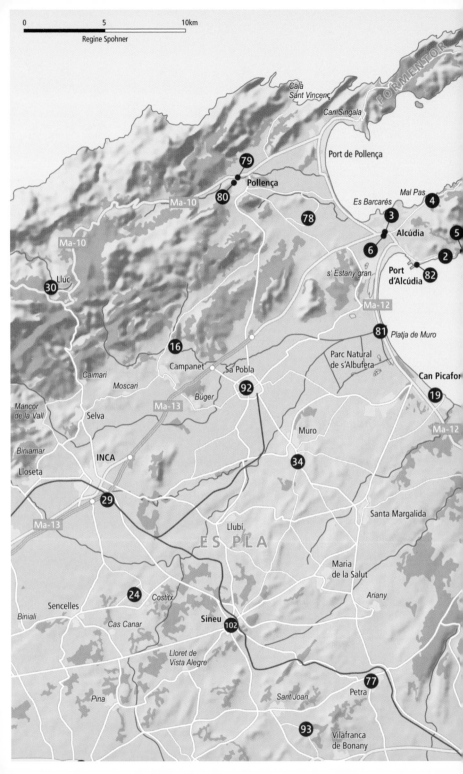

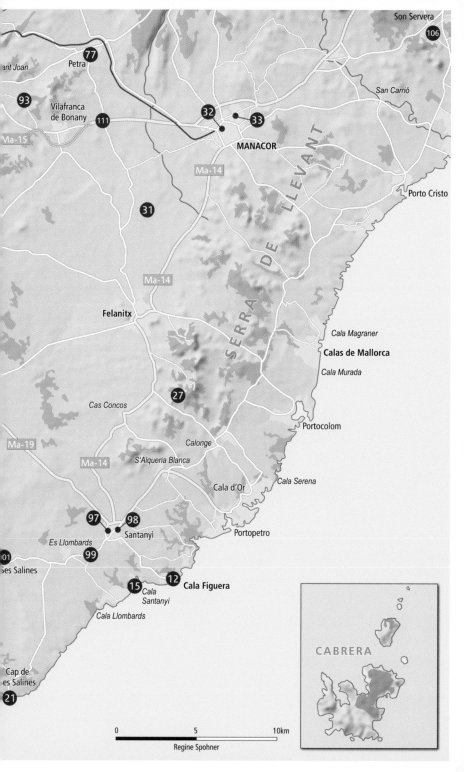

Son Servera

106

77 Petra

ant Joan

93

Vilafranca
de Bonany

111

Ma-15

32

33

MANACOR

San Carrió

SERRA DE LLEVANT

Ma-14

Porto Cristo

31

Ma-14

Cala Magraner

Calas de Mallorca

Felanitx

Cala Murada

27

Cas Concos

Portocolom

Calonge

Cala Serena

Ma-19

S'Alqueria Blanca

Ma-14

Cala d'Or

97 98

Santanyí

Portopetro

Es Llombards

99

01

es Salines

15 Cala
Santanyí

12 **Cala Figuera**

Cala Llombards

Cap de
es Salines

21

CABRERA

0   5   10km

Regine Spohner